C000174137

CONCEPT CARS
AND PROTOTYPES

CONCEPT CARS

AND PROTOTYPES

CONCEPT CAR DESIGN: EXPLORING THE FUTURE OF THE AUTOMOBILE

RICHARD DREDGE

Grange
BOOKS

Copyright © 2007 Amber Books Ltd

This edition first published in 2007 for Grange Books
An imprint of Grange Books Ltd
The Grange
Kingsnorth Industrial Estate
Hoo, nr Rochester
Kent ME3 9ND
www.grangebooks.co.uk

ISBN 978-1-84013-954-9

Editorial and design by
Amber Books Ltd
Bradley's Close
74–77 White Lion Street
London N1 9PF
www.amberbooks.co.uk

All images courtesy of Richard Dredge

Printed in Singapore

CONTENTS

INTRODUCTION

Back in the 1920s, there were some who thought that car design couldn't possibly advance. After three decades of evolution, cars were more reliable, more comfortable and more affordable than ever. Thankfully, some feel there is always room for improvement, which is why the boundaries continue to be pushed and cars get ever safer, faster, more reliable and comfortable. What's more, glimpses of our motoring future can be snatched by looking at the concept cars that are regularly wheeled out at motor shows worldwide – which prove that there's still a huge amount of progress to be made.

While few concepts make it into production, elements of many eventually reach the showrooms. Virtually anything can be promised, but everybody in the motor trade knows that manufacturers won't have to deliver on their promises because these are just ideas cars. It's all about fashion, which means that it's not until you've gone too far that you know just how far you can go. While many concepts are hardly what you could call adventurous, there are some that are decidedly challenging.

It has been decades now since the first 'dream car' was officially unveiled, and while it may not seem especially advanced in the twenty-first century, that first concept was of enormous significance. It set a standard and raised

Above: *The Lexus 2054 concept, which had a starring role in the 2002 Tom Cruise movie* Minority Report.

Above: Sadly never to be seen on the roads, Mercedes' C112 harked back to its 1970s concept cars and introduced some remarkable new technology that would eventually find its way into production models.

expectations forever – no longer would a rehashed version of last year's model be good enough. This first concept car was the 1938 Buick Y Job. Designed by Harley Earl of General Motors, this was a car which owed nothing to what had gone before – it was smooth, sleek, aerodynamic and impossibly stylish. It also remained a one-off, as it was simply too daring for pre-war car buyers.

While the Y Job is credited with being the first true concept car, half a decade before Buick's creation was first seen, a test-bed from Volvo was shown. This concept was created by an independent coach builder using a Volvo PV653 chassis, and was known as the Venus Bilo. When it was unveiled in November 1933, Volvo claimed to have no involvement in the project, but it was later disclosed that the car had been built to test reactions to its advanced styling – so it truly was a concept car.

Things have advanced enormously since the introduction of the Y Job in 1938. Now we routinely see concepts with new methods of propulsion, new bodystyles, innovative transmissions and mind-bending levels of equipment. Long may it continue.

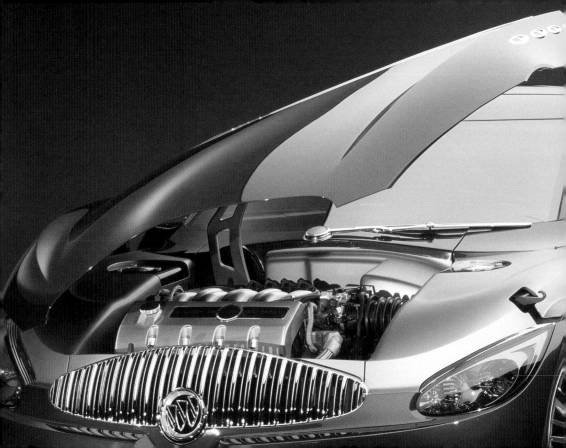

THE NEARLY CARS

Many of the concepts in this chapter could so easily have made it into production – and indeed many were originally intended to be offered for sale. In some instances, all that was needed was a greater sense of adventure and some faith; however, car manufacturers are notoriously conservative and projects that might just become icons are instead dropped, to be forgotten for ever.

In these pages are examples of cars that should have reached showrooms – either because they were nearly there anyway or because they were sufficiently different for it to be worth investing some effort in properly engineering them for sale. Such cars include the Audi Avantissimo, Chevrolet Nomad and Jaguar R-D6; they would have improved their makers' fortunes, and in some cases they would also have cornered the market by creating a new sector.

As well as the ones that should have made it, there are some which easily could have been engineered for production, but which thankfully were not. Cars such as the Buick Signia and Saturn CV-1 may have looked as though they were nearly there, but were so ugly that it's doubtful they would have found many buyers. Which just goes to show that sometimes manufacturers do get it right.

Left: *This sideways-hinged bonnet (hood) was just one of the innovations incorporated in the Buick LaCrosse, another automotive also-ran.*

ALFA ROMEO NUVOLA

The Nuvola may not have looked especially modern inside or out, but under the skin there was some radical technology. The car was built to show how easy it would be to return to the pre-war days of coach building on a separate chassis, although the Nuvola's platform was rather more advanced than the cars of several decades earlier. Mixing old with new, the shape was evocative of post-war coach-built specials, yet the technology incorporated was much more modern. Perhaps the most futuristic aspect was the lighting, which was compact and efficient; already seen on Alfa Romeo's GTV and Spider, it still looked cutting edge when it was unveiled.

SPECIFICATIONS

ENGINE CAPACITY:	2492 cc twin-turbo
CONFIGURATION:	front-mounted V6
POWER:	petrol
TOP SPEED:	224 kW (300 bhp)
TRANSMISSION:	267 km/h (166 mph)
	six-speed manual,
	four-wheel drive
LENGTH:	4286 mm (168.74 in)
WIDTH:	1859 mm (73.19 in)
DEBUT:	Paris 1996
DESIGNER:	Walter de Silva

The interior of the Nuvola, like the car's exterior, was a mix of old and new. The materials and designs were traditional, but the technology was modern.

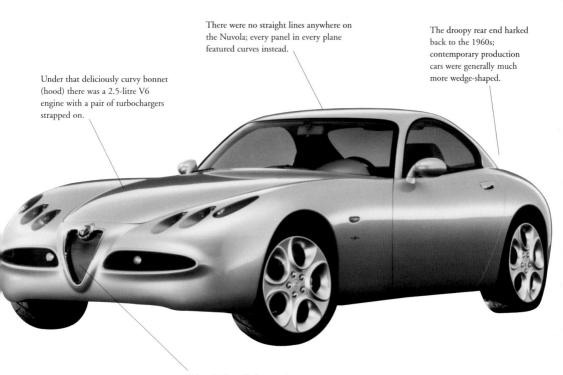

There were no straight lines anywhere on the Nuvola; every panel in every plane featured curves instead.

The droopy rear end harked back to the 1960s; contemporary production cars were generally much more wedge-shaped.

Under that deliciously curvy bonnet (hood) there was a 2.5-litre V6 engine with a pair of turbochargers strapped on.

Although the grille betrays the Nuvola's origins very clearly, it's those alloy wheels that offer the strongest corporate identity.

11

AUDI AVANTISSIMO

Although there have long been plenty of executive estates (station wagons) to choose from, truly luxurious ultra-spacious load-luggers have always been few and far between. The Avantissimo was Audi's attempt at filling this void, with generous performance, masses of equipment and acres of space. There was serious talk of the car going into production shortly after the car's debut in 2001; it would effectively have been an A8 Avant. Although the car would have had no rivals, Audi clearly decided that manufacturers such as Mercedes and BMW were holding back for a good reason. As a result, the Avantissimo never saw the light of day in production form.

SPECIFICATIONS

ENGINE CAPACITY:	4.2-litre twin-turbo
CONFIGURATION:	front-mounted V8 petrol
POWER:	321 kW (430 bhp)
TOP SPEED:	250 km/h (155 mph) (limited)
TRANSMISSION:	six-speed semi-auto, four-wheel drive
LENGTH:	5060 mm (199.21 in)
WIDTH:	1910 mm (75.20 in)
DEBUT:	Frankfurt 2001

The Avantissimo's interior was incredibly luxurious, with plenty of leather and Alcantara in evidence – along with equipment galore.

The tyres were run-flat Michelin Pax items, while there were also pressure sensors at each corner to warn of any deflation.

In a bid to keep weight down, the bodyshell was made entirely of aluminium – although this was still a heavy car.

With conservative lines, the Avantissimo looked like a grown-up A6 Avant – those Audi corporate design cues meant that it could be easily identified.

In the nose was a 4.2-litre V8 engine, capable of developing up to 321 kW (430 bhp). The power went to all four wheels.

BERTONE BIRUSA

B ertone claimed that putting the Birusa into production wouldn't take much effort, but we're still waiting. It's unlikely anything similar will reach production because so many of the details are expensive solutions to straightforward problems. Those electrically assisted doors look fabulous when open – but they're costly to engineer. Almost the entire upper section was glass, so climate control had to be fitted. There was also a voice-activation system to control many of the car's major functions. Joining in the techno-fest was Bose, which supplied a top-end stereo system to bathe the car's occupants in music. The grand finale was the facility to carry a Segway Human Transporter in the boot.

SPECIFICATIONS

ENGINE CAPACITY:	4941 cc
CONFIGURATION:	front-mounted V8 petrol
POWER:	298 kW (400 bhp)
TOP SPEED:	n/a
TRANSMISSION:	six-speed manual, rear-wheel drive
LENGTH:	4400 mm (173.23 in)
WIDTH:	1900 mm (74.80 in)
DEBUT:	Geneva 2003

While it is true that the exterior design of the Birusa initially looks simple, it's certainly not bland. If you look closely, there's something new to see each time.

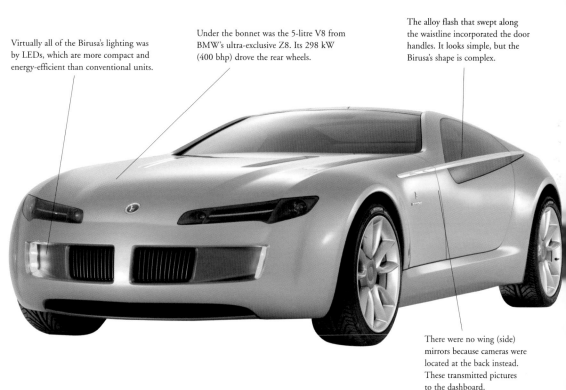

Virtually all of the Birusa's lighting was by LEDs, which are more compact and energy-efficient than conventional units.

Under the bonnet was the 5-litre V8 from BMW's ultra-exclusive Z8. Its 298 kW (400 bhp) drove the rear wheels.

The alloy flash that swept along the waistline incorporated the door handles. It looks simple, but the Birusa's shape is complex.

There were no wing (side) mirrors because cameras were located at the back instead. These transmitted pictures to the dashboard.

BERTONE ZABRUS

Take one Group B rally special, remove its bodyshell, then build an altogether more practical car on what's left. That's what Bertone did with its 1986 Zabrus, when it borrowed a Citroën BX 4TC and worked its magic to come up with the Zabrus concept for the Turin motor show. While the mechanics were borrowed from the Citroën, the engine was detuned for greater reliability and tractability. Attempting to offer a mix of practicality and style in the mould of the Reliant Scimitar GTE, the Zabrus was a three-door sporting estate (station wagon). That was tasteful enough – but the kangaroo-skin interior definitely wasn't …

SPECIFICATIONS

ENGINE CAPACITY:	2141 cc turbocharged
CONFIGURATION:	front-mounted in-line four petrol
POWER:	149 kW (200 bhp)
TOP SPEED:	222 km/h (138 mph)
TRANSMISSION:	five-speed manual, four-wheel drive
LENGTH:	4300 mm (169.29 in)
WIDTH:	1880 mm (74.02 in)
DEBUT:	Turin 1986

A CD player was fitted in the dash; it was envisaged that one day this would allow satellite navigation to be offered. Bertone claimed a car's interior should be ornate like that of a house, hence the mosaic incorporated within the car's headlining.

The Zabrus was meant to be an ultra-safe car, so the driver's seat automatically adjusted for maximum visibility.

The instrumentation was displayed in such a way that drivers barely needed to take their eyes off the road.

The doors opened with a scissor action – hardly practical, but guaranteed to look good on the motor-show stand.

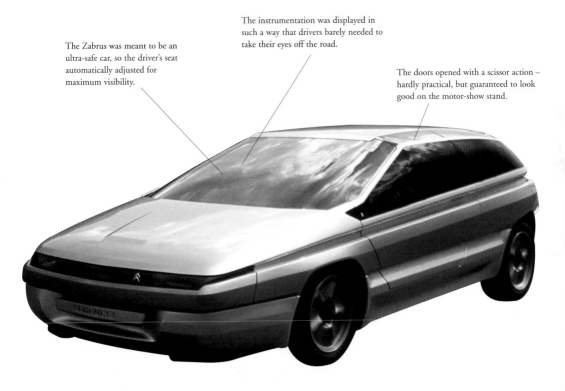

BUICK LACROSSE

The LaCrosse suffered from something of an identity crisis in that it could be converted from a saloon to a pick-up or even a convertible – all at the touch of a button. As Buick put it, the LaCrosse was a 'master of metamorphosis', although its primary aim was to offer luxurious travel for five. To that end there was plenty of space inside, but more importantly there was just about every possible piece of equipment shoehorned into the cabin. There were also plenty of expensive materials, and, while the interior design was something to savour, the exterior styling most definitely wasn't.

SPECIFICATIONS

ENGINE CAPACITY:	4.2 litres
CONFIGURATION:	front-mounted V8 petrol
POWER:	198 kW (265 bhp)
TOP SPEED:	n/a
TRANSMISSION:	four-speed auto, front-wheel drive
LENGTH:	5192 mm (204.41 in)
WIDTH:	1952 mm (76.85 in)
DEBUT:	Detroit 2000
DESIGNERS:	Benjamin Jiminez Yuntae Kim

The LaCrosse had a huge amount of equipment fitted, including a telephone, satellite navigation and a head-up display.

In saloon form there was a huge glass roof fitted; this could be retracted to turn the car into a convertible.

Considering that the LaCrosse could ultimately be turned into a pick-up, its looks were surprisingly aggressive for such a utilitarian vehicle.

With the LaCrosse hailing from America, there was only one type of engine that could be fitted in the nose: a petrol-fed V8.

Most of the car's equipment was voice-activated, with a joystick used to control everything – much like BMW's iDrive system.

BUICK SIGNIA

Looking almost as horrifically disfigured as the Pontiac Aztek, the Buick Signia was never going to win any prizes for its ungainly looks. While those on the outside may have pointed and stared, those on the inside at least had the opportunity to travel in comfort thanks to the generous levels of equipment, high-quality materials and large quantities of space on offer. This was Buick's attempt at showing it could produce a premium family estate (station wagon) that would get buyers out of their BMWs and Audis, and back to buying American once more. The problem was that, while the Signia proved the comfort was there, the design clearly wasn't.

SPECIFICATIONS

ENGINE CAPACITY:	3800 cc supercharged
CONFIGURATION:	front-mounted petrol V6
POWER:	179 kW (240 bhp)
TOP SPEED:	n/a
TRANSMISSION:	four-speed auto, part-time four-wheel drive
LENGTH:	4705 mm (185.24 in)
WIDTH:	1886 mm (74.25 in)
DEBUT:	Detroit 1998

Flexibility was an important aspect of the Signia, so the tailgate could be removed for bulky objects, while the load bay floor extended rearwards.

Easy access was one of the keys to the Signia's design, hence the tall roof and the high seats front and rear.

The Signia used Buick's production Park Avenue saloon as its basis, complete with either front- or four-wheel drive.

Drivers could log in and everything would set automatically: seat and steering wheel positions, plus climate control and audio settings.

Only the front wheels were driven in normal driving; however, if slip was detected at the back wheels, electric motors kicked in.

CADILLAC AURORA

During the 1980s and 1990s, Cadillac built a fantastic range of radical concepts that started with the Voyage, progressed through the Solitaire and ended with the Aurora. If only Cadillac had possessed the courage to be more radical with its production cars. With its pronounced wedge shape and flush glazing, the Aurora and its predecessors were meant to entice younger buyers out of their European cars. The running gear was pure Americana, however, as it was a 4.5-litre V8 hooked up to a four-speed automatic gearbox. While that didn't promise a very sporting drive, Cadillac said any production cars would have a six-speed manual transmission instead.

SPECIFICATIONS

ENGINE CAPACITY:	4467 cc
CONFIGURATION:	front-mounted petrol V8
POWER:	149 kW (200 bhp)
TOP SPEED:	n/a
TRANSMISSION:	four-speed automatic, four-wheel drive
LENGTH:	4849 mm (190.91 in)
WIDTH:	1880 mm (74.02 in)
DEBUT:	Detroit 1990

The whole of the Aurora's bodyshell was made of glassfibre, for ease of construction. Production cars would have been steel.

Cadillac shunned tradition with the Aurora's exterior, which is why there was no chrome, to make it look sportier.

The sunroof featured a liquid crystal that could be adjusted by the driver, to allow more or less light through.

The four-speed automatic transmission that was fitted would have been swapped for a six-speed manual unit in the event of production.

Although the interior was very comfortable with its wraparound fascia, it was also largely conventional in its design.

23

CHEVROLET NOMAD

There have been no fewer than three Nomad concepts from Chevrolet, the first arriving in 1954 and based on the Corvette. It wasn't until 1999 that there was a follow-up; by 2004 the name was used again for this small load carrier based on the company's Kappa platform. The reason for this Nomad's size was the unexpected success of the Mini in the United States: it seemed that small no longer meant an automatic sales handicap. The Nomad was designed to appeal to drivers of any age, just like the Mini – and, just like that car, there was plenty of space inside despite the diminutive proportions.

SPECIFICATIONS

ENGINE CAPACITY:	2200 cc turbocharged
CONFIGURATION:	front-mounted in-line four-cylinder petrol
POWER:	186 kW (250 bhp)
TOP SPEED:	n/a
TRANSMISSION:	five-speed semi-auto, rear-wheel drive
LENGTH:	3950 mm (155.51 in)
WIDTH:	1700 mm (66.93 in)
DEBUT:	Detroit 2004
DESIGNER:	Simon Cox

Practicality was key to the Nomad, with all sorts of interior configurations possible. The result was carrying ability that belied the compact dimensions.

Previous Nomads had been built to typical oversized American dimensions, but this new car was far smaller.

Transmitting the 186 kW (250 bhp) to the back was a five-speed gearbox with fully automatic or sequential manual modes.

Those 508-mm (20-in) wheels were ridiculously oversized. But they looked great with the ultra low-profile tyres.

For a car of this size, the 2.2-litre turbocharged engine offered a lot of power. With rear-wheel drive it would be superb to drive.

FERRARI PININ

While Porsche has strayed from its natural habitat to build an off-roader and Maserati also briefly toyed with the thought of one, Ferrari has never offered anything so mundane as a four-door saloon. If it had done so, the Pinin would surely have been deserving of the prancing-horse badge; this was one cutting-edge car when it was first shown in 1980. While performance was the order of the day thanks to a 5-litre flat-12 engine up front, there was also luxury. So far Ferrari has stayed with two doors, but with Porsche and Aston Martin both set to offer four-door saloons, maybe it's only a matter of time …

SPECIFICATIONS

ENGINE CAPACITY:	4942 cc
CONFIGURATION:	front-mounted flat-12
POWER:	268 kW (360 bhp)
TOP SPEED:	n/a
TRANSMISSION:	five-speed manual, rear-wheel drive
LENGTH:	5050 mm (198.82 in)
WIDTH:	1816 mm (71.50 in)
DEBUT:	Turin 1980

To ensure the Pinin was ultra-slippery, there was flush glazing all round; the windows were sealed shut as well.

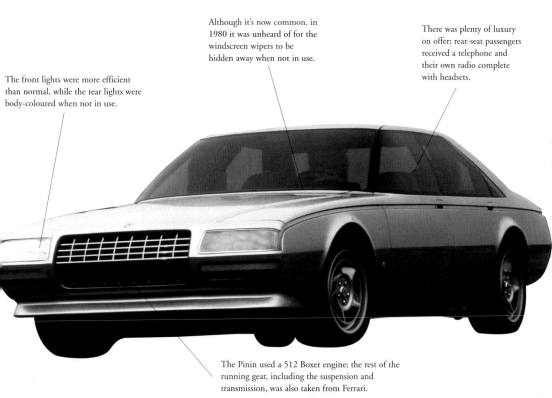

The front lights were more efficient than normal, while the rear lights were body-coloured when not in use.

Although it's now common, in 1980 it was unheard of for the windscreen wipers to be hidden away when not in use.

There was plenty of luxury on offer; rear-seat passengers received a telephone and their own radio complete with headsets.

The Pinin used a 512 Boxer engine; the rest of the running gear, including the suspension and transmission, was also taken from Ferrari.

GHIA FOCUS

Wholly owned by Ford, Turin-based Ghia designs many of the former's concept cars; sometimes they wear Ghia badges and sometimes the Blue Oval. In this case there was a Ghia badge on the nose, but the mechanicals were pure Ford, thanks to the Escort Cosworth donating its vital organs. Intended to be a sports car for the 1990s, the Focus mixed organic tones with natural materials – even the floor was wooden. However, the bodyshell was more cutting edge than that, as it was created from composites for the optimum balance of strength and lightness. There was talk of the car reaching production, but it sadly didn't happen.

SPECIFICATIONS

ENGINE CAPACITY:	1994 cc
CONFIGURATION:	front-mounted in-line petrol four-cylinder
POWER:	172 kW (230 bhp)
TOP SPEED:	241 km/h (150 mph)
TRANSMISSION:	five-speed manual, four-wheel drive
LENGTH:	4135 mm (162.79 in)
WIDTH:	1793 mm (70.59 in)
DEBUT:	Geneva 1992
DESIGNER:	Taru Lahti

There wasn't a straight line to be found on the Ghia Focus, with all of the bodywork being crafted from carbon fibre for lightness.

The interior used as many natural materials as possible, such as wood and leather. The seats resembled saddles.

The grey colour scheme was chosen so that people would concentrate on the car's lines, rather than a glitzy finish.

tead of a conventional aust pipe at the rear, re was a 'spark arrester' ilar to those used on he off-roaders.

With all the mechanicals from the Escort Cosworth, the only departure from standard was the adoption of 457-mm (18-in) alloy wheels.

GMC TERRADYNE

Genral Motors' designers came over all multicultural with their 2000 Terradyne concept. With 'terra' being taken from the Latin for earth and 'dyne' being Greek for strength and power, this full-sized pick-up truck featured aggressive styling, a hint of utilitarianism and a healthy dose of innovation. After nearly a century of building pick-up trucks, GMC knew a thing or two about what made a decent one. As a result, the Terradyne could be used comfortably as everyday family transport or stacked up with building materials without complaint. The problem was fuel prices were making such leviathans deeply unfashionable at the time …

SPECIFICATIONS

ENGINE CAPACITY:	6.6 litres
CONFIGURATION:	front-mounted V8 turbodiesel
POWER:	224 kW (300 bhp)
TOP SPEED:	n/a
TRANSMISSION:	five-speed auto, four-wheel drive
LENGTH:	5723 mm (225.31 in)
WIDTH:	2057 mm (80.98 in)
DEBUT:	Detroit 2000
DESIGNER:	Carl Zipfel

The Terradyne's load bay was usually 1.83 m (six feet) long, but this could be extended electrically by 61 cm (two feet) for bulky items.

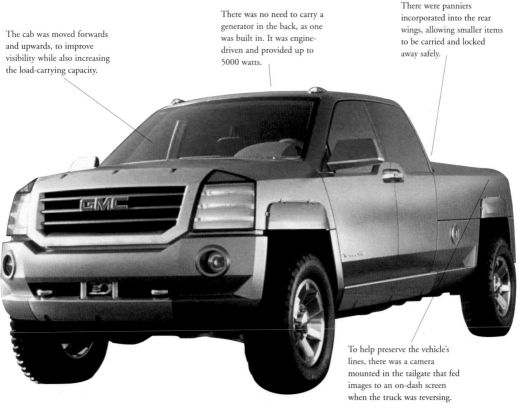

The cab was moved forwards and upwards, to improve visibility while also increasing the load-carrying capacity.

There was no need to carry a generator in the back, as one was built in. It was engine-driven and provided up to 5000 watts.

There were panniers incorporated into the rear wings, allowing smaller items to be carried and locked away safely.

To help preserve the vehicle's lines, there was a camera mounted in the tailgate that fed images to an on-dash screen when the truck was reversing.

JAGUAR R-D6

W e'd heard it before with the R Coupé, but this time it would be different. Here was the start of a new era for Jaguar, with not only a new bodystyle for the company (a five-door hatchback), but also a new form of motive power. Using the bi-turbo V6 diesel engine that would go on to power both the S-Type and the XJ, the R-D6 was based on the platform of the latter. Like that car, it was also built of aluminium to keep weight down – but the design was much more radical with those rear-hinged back doors and ultra-short overhangs. We're still waiting …

SPECIFICATIONS

ENGINE CAPACITY:	2.7-litre twin-turbo
CONFIGURATION:	front-engined V6 diesel
POWER:	172 kW (230 bhp)
TOP SPEED:	249 km/h (155 mph)
TRANSMISSION:	five-speed auto
LENGTH:	4330 mm (170.47 in)
WIDTH:	2150 mm (84.65 in)
DEBUT:	Frankfurt 2003
DESIGNERS:	Matt Beaven
	Alister Whelan

Composites and aluminium were used extensively in the construction, but the final weight was still a hefty 1500 kg (3307 lb) because of all the equipment.

Composites and aluminium were used extensively in the construction, but the final weight was still a hefty 1500 kg (3307 lb) because of all the equipment.

Although Jaguar's expertise lay in building highly refined cars powered by petrol engines, the R-D6 packed a turbocharged V6 diesel unit up front, which was rated at 172 kW (230 bhp).

Those spoked wheels were 533 mm (21 in) across, and they were wrapped in 30-profile tyres – an even lower profile than most other concepts.

It looks like a two-door coupé, but the R-D6 is a five-door hatch. The tailgate was side-hinged – like the E-Type's.

LAGONDA VIGNALE

Although some accused the Lagonda Vignale of looking like nothing more than a rehashed Jaguar Mk2, most who saw the car reckoned it was one of the concepts that really shouldn't have been allowed to get away. Here was a car that could have given the Mercedes S-Class and BMW 7-Series a run for their money – but the Vignale also served a decent helping of style at the same time. Styled by Ghia, the Vignale was essentially a Ford confection. Initially there was talk of the Vignale making production, and at first it seemed there was no shortage of buyers. Sadly, Ford decided that the sums didn't add up.

The interior of the Vignale was fabulously ornate, with strong art deco overtones and masses of wood, leather and alloy in evidence.

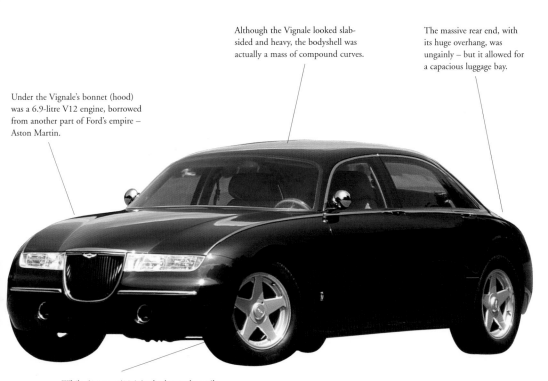

Although the Vignale looked slab-sided and heavy, the bodyshell was actually a mass of compound curves.

The massive rear end, with its huge overhang, was ungainly – but it allowed for a capacious luggage bay.

Under the Vignale's bonnet (hood) was a 6.9-litre V12 engine, borrowed from another part of Ford's empire – Aston Martin.

While 483-mm (19-in) wheels may be easily available nowadays, when the Vignale was unveiled they were virtually unheard of.

LAMBORGHINI FLYING STAR II

T here may never have been a Lamborghini Flying Star I, but Carrozzeria Touring did build a series of cars in the 1930s wearing such a badge. This was the same company that built the 400GT on Lamborghini's behalf, and the coach builder spotted an opportunity for a special body based on what was then Lamborghini's main production car. Dubbed the Flying Star II, it was hoped this would lead to a contract to build the 400GT's successor, but it wasn't to be. As a result, only that initial car was made. Although the Flying Star II doesn't look very radical – or especially sporting – it was advanced for its time.

SPECIFICATIONS

ENGINE CAPACITY:	3929 cc
CONFIGURATION:	front-mounted V12
POWER:	239 kW (320 bhp)
TOP SPEED:	249 km/h (155 mph)
TRANSMISSION:	five-speed manual, rear-wheel drive
LENGTH:	4380 mm (172.44 in)
WIDTH:	1720 mm (67.72 in)
DEBUT:	Turin 1966

Although it was more overtly sporting, the Flying Star II was nonetheless a fast three-door estate (station wagon) like the Volvo 1800ES and the Reliant Scimitar GTE.

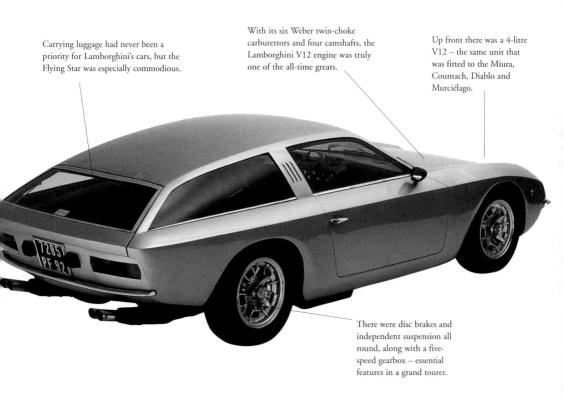

Carrying luggage had never been a priority for Lamborghini's cars, but the Flying Star was especially commodious.

With its six Weber twin-choke carburettors and four camshafts, the Lamborghini V12 engine was truly one of the all-time greats.

Up front there was a 4-litre V12 – the same unit that was fitted to the Miura, Countach, Diablo and Murciélago.

There were disc brakes and independent suspension all round, along with a five-speed gearbox – essential features in a grand tourer.

MG E-XE

The British-owned motor industry has produced relatively few concept cars over the years, but when one does get built it tends to be worth waiting for. The non-running MG E-XE was just such a concept – by the time the car made its debut in 1985, the MG marque seemed to be on its last legs. The MG B had been axed years earlier, and the only presence MG had was due to badge-engineered cars such as the Metro, Maestro and Montego. What was needed was a shot in the arm to show that there was still life in the company – and that's exactly what the E-XE delivered.

SPECIFICATIONS

ENGINE CAPACITY:	2991 cc
CONFIGURATION:	mid-mounted V6 petrol
POWER:	186 kW (250 bhp)
TOP SPEED:	275 km/h (171 mph)
TRANSMISSION:	five-speed manual, four-wheel drive
LENGTH:	n/a
WIDTH:	n/a
DEBUT:	Frankfurt 1985
DESIGNER:	Roy Axe, Gordon Sked

Inside there was plenty of equipment such as satellite navigation, but it was only a mock-up because the technology didn't exist for it to work.

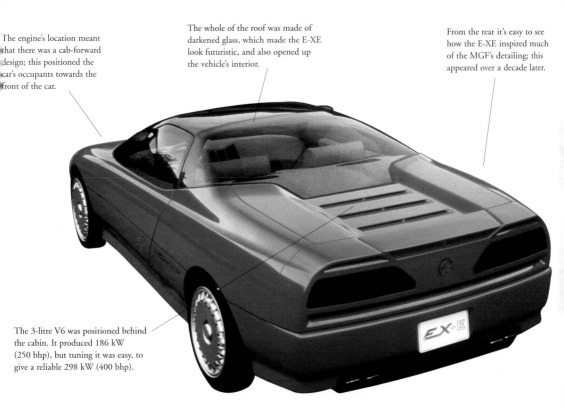

The engine's location meant that there was a cab-forward design; this positioned the car's occupants towards the front of the car.

The whole of the roof was made of darkened glass, which made the E-XE look futuristic, and also opened up the vehicle's interior.

From the rear it's easy to see how the E-XE inspired much of the MGF's detailing; this appeared over a decade later.

The 3-litre V6 was positioned behind the cabin. It produced 186 kW (250 bhp), but tuning it was easy, to give a reliable 298 kW (400 bhp).

NISSAN URGE

The Urge was born from an on-line survey that Nissan conducted into the buying habits of young Americans, which concluded that performance and technology were their key requirements. Something that was fun to drive was needed, but it had to incorporate such gadgets as a mobile phone, MP3 player and games console – while also being affordable. It was the games console that was foremost in the designers' minds, with several of the styling cues revolving around this. With a sense of adventure being a part of the gamer's make-up, the Urge was intended to be a bit off-the-wall, while also being real-world enough to be usable as an everyday driver.

SPECIFICATIONS

ENGINE CAPACITY:	n/a
CONFIGURATION:	front-mounted
POWER:	six-speed semi-auto, rear-wheel drive
TOP SPEED:	n/a
TRANSMISSION:	six-speed semi-auto, rear-wheel drive
LENGTH:	3979 mm (156.65 in)
WIDTH:	1824 mm (71.81 in)
DEBUT:	Detroit 2006

The Nissan Urge's exposed exterior and heavily flared wheelarches were reminiscent of a motorcycle, as was the alloy centre structure.

Nissan didn't specify what engine was fitted, but it claimed the powerplant would be a high-revving small-displacement unit.

For maximum agility and performance, weight was kept to a minimum; the kerb weight was just over a ton at 1091 kg (2405 lb).

A semiautomatic gearbox was fitted, which allowed the driver to choose each of the six ratios sequentially.

As with all the best driver's cars, it was the rear wheels that were driven, but the engine was mounted at the front.

PLYMOUTH PRONTO SPYDER

At first glance this car looked just like a Porsche Boxster; however, unlike the boys in Stuttgart, Plymouth tragically didn't have the courage to put its Pronto Spyder into production. Engineered as a fully running prototype, Plymouth reckoned it could offer its car for sale at half the price of a Boxster or Mercedes SLK. The secret was to use the plastic from recycled drink bottles – which didn't need painting and could be recycled once again when the car was finished with. It was claimed this could cut the cost of building the cars by as much as 80 per cent – but this clearly still wasn't enough, as the car was never offered for sale.

SPECIFICATIONS

ENGINE CAPACITY:	2429 cc supercharged
CONFIGURATION:	mid-mounted in-line four-cylinder petrol
POWER:	168 kW (225 bhp)
TOP SPEED:	225 km/h (140 mph)
TRANSMISSION:	five-speed manual, rear-wheel drive
LENGTH:	3926 mm (154.57 in)
WIDTH:	1753 mm (69.02 in)
DEBUT:	Detroit 1998
DESIGNER:	Mike Castiglione

In addition to a tortoiseshell steering-wheel rim there were sprung spokes, while the instrument panel was engine-turned aluminium.

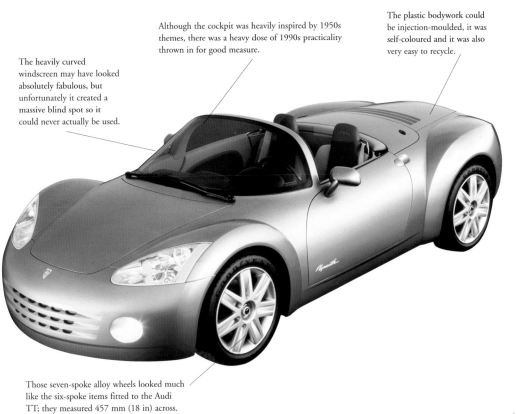

The heavily curved windscreen may have looked absolutely fabulous, but unfortunately it created a massive blind spot so it could never actually be used.

Although the cockpit was heavily inspired by 1950s themes, there was a heavy dose of 1990s practicality thrown in for good measure.

The plastic bodywork could be injection-moulded, it was self-coloured and it was also very easy to recycle.

Those seven-spoke alloy wheels looked much like the six-spoke items fitted to the Audi TT; they measured 457 mm (18 in) across.

RENAULT FIFTIE

The Fiftie was produced to mark half a century since the introduction of the Renault 4CV, the car of choice for the middle classes in post-war France. That's why the concept was heavily inspired by the production car of 50 years earlier, although there were a lot of neat touches which ensured the 1996 car was rather more contemporary. The greatest tragedy was that the Fiftie was never put into production – even if it had been produced in small numbers, it would surely have been popular enough be built at a profit. It could even have become the European equivalent of Nissan's retro Figaro, built on the Micra platform.

SPECIFICATIONS

ENGINE CAPACITY:	1149 cc
CONFIGURATION:	mid-mounted in-line four petrol
POWER:	45 kW (60 bhp)
TOP SPEED:	n/a
TRANSMISSION:	five-speed semi-auto, rear-wheel drive
LENGTH:	n/a
WIDTH:	n/a
DEBUT:	Geneva 1996
DESIGNER:	Benoit Jacob

The car's lines were based on those of the post-war 4CV, which compromised the packaging because of the mechanical layout.

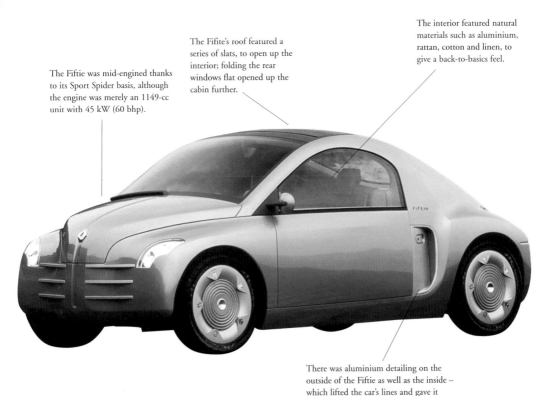

The Fiftie was mid-engined thanks to its Sport Spider basis, although the engine was merely an 1149-cc unit with 45 kW (60 bhp).

The Fifite's roof featured a series of slats, to open up the interior; folding the rear windows flat opened up the cabin further.

The interior featured natural materials such as aluminium, rattan, cotton and linen, to give a back-to-basics feel.

There was aluminium detailing on the outside of the Fiftie as well as the inside – which lifted the car's lines and gave it a contemporary look.

SATURN CV-1

As the name suggests, the CV-1 was the first concept vehicle to come from Saturn, and it was launched at the 2000 Detroit motor show. The focus was on practicality, with a high roof, a spacious load bay and a novel door arrangement that was almost certainly too complicated for its own good. With its simple interior and flexible seating arrangement, the CV-1 would certainly have made a lot of sense for a huge number of buyers. As well as the functional aspects, there were some neat features packed into the CV-1 – it's just a shame that the thing looked so terminally dull.

SPECIFICATIONS

ENGINE CAPACITY:	2.2 litres
CONFIGURATION:	front-mounted in-line four-cylinder petrol
POWER:	102 kW (137 bhp)
TOP SPEED:	n/a
TRANSMISSION:	CVT, four-wheel drive
LENGTH:	4496 mm (177.01 in)
WIDTH:	1778 mm (70 in)
DEBUT:	Detroit 2000

Up to five people could be carried in the CV-1, with the front passenger and two rear rows of seats able to fold flat into the floor.

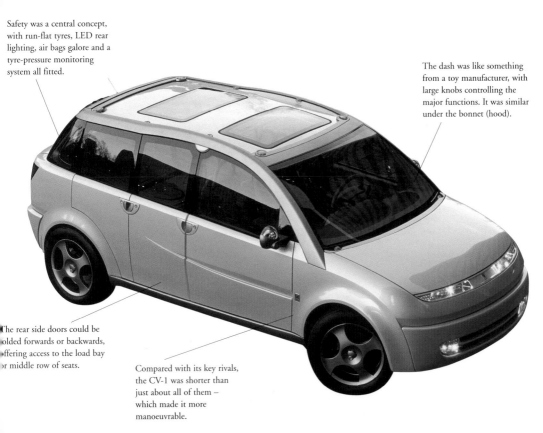

Safety was a central concept, with run-flat tyres, LED rear lighting, air bags galore and a tyre-pressure monitoring system all fitted.

The dash was like something from a toy manufacturer, with large knobs controlling the major functions. It was similar under the bonnet (hood).

The rear side doors could be folded forwards or backwards, offering access to the load bay or middle row of seats.

Compared with its key rivals, the CV-1 was shorter than just about all of them – which made it more manoeuvrable.

SATURN CURVE

Big news at the 2004 Detroit motor show was GM's new Kappa platform, which would enable it to produce a diverse range of cars without the need for costly re-engineering each time. To prove the point, the Pontiac Solstice, Chevrolet Nomad and Saturn Curve were all rolled out; they were a convertible, an estate car (station wagon) and a coupé, respectively. They all shared similar dimensions and each packed the same mechanicals in terms of engine, transmission, brakes and suspension. All looked fabulous, and there was a front engine and rear-wheel drive in each case. While the Curve didn't make it into production, at least the Solstice did.

SPECIFICATIONS

ENGINE CAPACITY:	2200 cc
CONFIGURATION:	front-mounted in-line four-cylinder supercharged petrol
POWER:	172 kW (230 bhp)
TOP SPEED:	n/a
TRANSMISSION:	five-speed manual, rear-wheel drive
LENGTH:	3975 mm (156.50 in)
WIDTH:	1811 mm (71.30 in)
DEBUT:	Detroit 2004

The Curve wasn't especially big or heavy, but there were 323-mm (12.72-in) brake discs at the front, along with 320-mm (12.60-in) units at the rear.

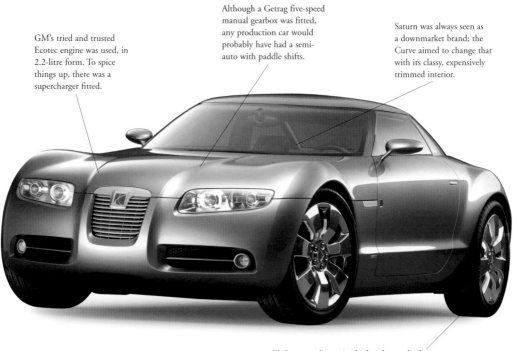

GM's tried and trusted Ecotec engine was used, in 2.2-litre form. To spice things up, there was a supercharger fitted.

Although a Getrag five-speed manual gearbox was fitted, any production car would probably have had a semi-auto with paddle shifts.

Saturn was always seen as a downmarket brand; the Curve aimed to change that with its classy, expensively trimmed interior.

To house such massive brakes, huge wheels were needed; they were seven-spoke items with a diameter of 508 mm (20 in).

SUBARU B11S

For a company that was synonymous with practical four-wheel-drive saloons and estates (station wagons), Subaru made a radical departure with the B11S. Although Subaru had a reputation for reliable and accessible performance – thanks largely to its Impreza Turbo – there had always been a large dose of practicality thrown into the mix. At first glance, the B11S (an abbreviation of Boxer 11 Sports) threw all that away, to focus instead on controversial design that put form before function. But look closely and you'll see that very little was sacrificed, yet the B11S still managed to be much more stylish than anything that Subaru had ever offered for sale.

SPECIFICATIONS

ENGINE CAPACITY:	3-litre twin-turbo
CONFIGURATION:	front-mounted flat-six
POWER:	petrol
	298 kW (400 bhp)
TOP SPEED:	n/a
TRANSMISSION:	five-speed auto, four-wheel drive
LENGTH:	4785 mm (188.39 in)
WIDTH:	1935 mm (76.18 in)
DEBUT:	Geneva 2003

The design of Subaru's B11S worked well overall, but the car's nose was less successful, with too much space given over to various grilles.

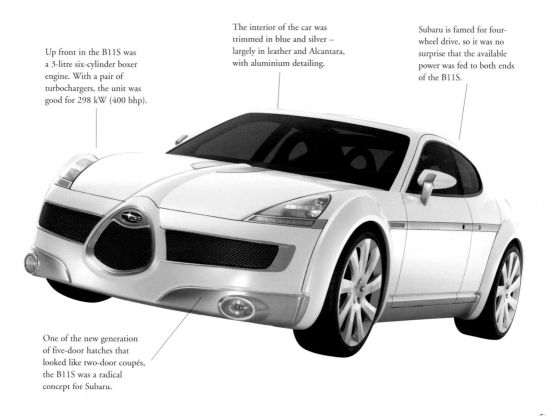

Up front in the B11S was a 3-litre six-cylinder boxer engine. With a pair of turbochargers, the unit was good for 298 kW (400 bhp).

The interior of the car was trimmed in blue and silver – largely in leather and Alcantara, with aluminium detailing.

Subaru is famed for four-wheel drive, so it was no surprise that the available power was fed to both ends of the B11S.

One of the new generation of five-door hatches that looked like two-door coupés, the B11S was a radical concept for Subaru.

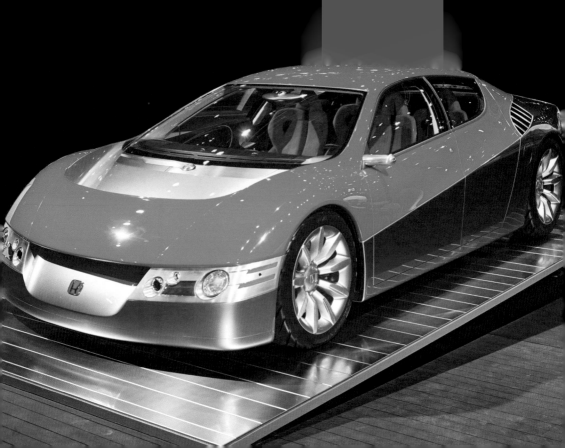

SAVING THE PLANET

As environmentalism takes a hold, car makers have to become more responsible for the impact of their cars on the planet and society. That's why car manufacturers are striving to build safer cars that are also cleaner and more fuel-efficient, with some radical solutions having to be found. This is where the real purpose of the concept car is evident – technologies that are first being seen on some of the more advanced show cars are making the leap to production cars, and in many cases are revolutionizing designs and construction processes.

While recyclable materials are being used in increasing concentrations in both concept and production cars, it's the way those cars are being designed and built that offer the most exciting possibilities for the future of transport. Vehicles such as GM's Hy-Wire show that, by embracing key technologies such as drive-by-wire, we can have safer cars that are also more efficient and far more comfortable.

Cars of the future will also have to clean up their act when it comes to motive power; many of the concepts in this chapter feature hybrid powertrains, fuel cells and battery packs. While the purely electric car will probably never happen on a large scale, there are exciting times ahead as far as powerplants are concerned.

Left: *The Honda Dualnote combined huge power with remarkable fuel efficiency, but proved too expensive to manufacture commercially.*

BMW E1

There were two E1 concepts from BMW; the first made its debut at the 1991 Frankfurt motor show, while the second followed two years later. They were both electrically powered commuter cars, and they each had the same problem – that of battery technology not being advanced enough to make the cars viable. To help overcome this, BMW developed the second E1 so it was available as a hybrid or even as a petrol-engined vehicle, albeit with a small powerplant to keep running costs to a minimum. In the event, the necessary breakthrough in battery technology has yet to be found, so BMW is sticking with the internal combustion engine.

SPECIFICATIONS

ENGINE CAPACITY:	electric motor
CONFIGURATION:	rear-mounted
POWER:	34 kW (45 bhp)
TOP SPEED:	121 km/h (75 mph)
TRANSMISSION:	direct drive, rear-wheel drive
LENGTH:	3460 mm (136.22 in)
WIDTH:	1648 mm (64.88 in)
DEBUT:	Frankfurt 1991

The interior of the E1 featured very little equipment or instrumentation, but it still looked classy thanks to the use of expensive materials.

To keep the weight as low as possible (to help increase the range), the bodywork was made of aluminium.

An electric motor was positioned between the rear wheels, to keep the centre of gravity as low as possible.

The E1 was kept short, with minimal overhangs front and rear. This made the car more manoeuvrable around town.

M·JE 9483

The E1 was very small, but it was packaged in such a way that there was room for a quartet of passengers.

CITROËN CITELA

Surprisingly few concept cars have relied on electricity for their motive power, but the Citela was one of them. When Citroën unveiled the car in 1991, the company fervently hoped that this could be the city car of the future – with four seats, a top speed of 113 km/h (70 mph) and a 209-km (130-mile) range. While other manufacturers had touted expensive or heavy battery solutions, Citroën reckoned it had everything sewn up with its nickel-hydride units. All it needed was the cooperation of the electricity companies, and urban environments could be transformed with fleets of electric vehicles. Sadly, the electricity companies didn't want to get involved.

SPECIFICATIONS

ENGINE CAPACITY:	six 12-volt batteries
CONFIGURATION:	n/a
POWER:	n/a
TOP SPEED:	113 km/h (70 mph)
TRANSMISSION:	n/a
LENGTH:	n/a
WIDTH:	n/a
DEBUT:	1991

The modular construction of the Citela meant that it would be easy to build a convertible, van, pick-up or estate (station wagon) on the same platform.

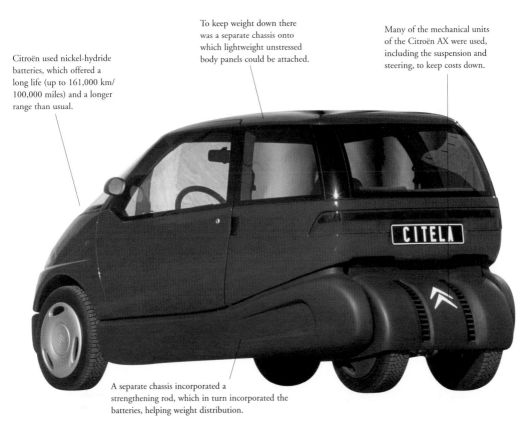

Citroën used nickel-hydride batteries, which offered a long life (up to 161,000 km/ 100,000 miles) and a longer range than usual.

To keep weight down there was a separate chassis onto which lightweight unstressed body panels could be attached.

Many of the mechanical units of the Citroën AX were used, including the suspension and steering, to keep costs down.

CITELA

A separate chassis incorporated a strengthening rod, which in turn incorporated the batteries, helping weight distribution.

DAIHATSU D-BONE

You can always rely on Daihatsu to come up with something barking mad, even if it's just a daft name. With the D being short for 'Dynamic' and the 'Bone' element coming from the fact that the car looked like a skeleton on wheels, Daihatsu reckoned that this was just what the youth of 2004 were after. It was a small, lightweight off-roader that would be cheap to run as well as to own – and in the caring, sharing 2000s, it would be kind to the environment, too. Well, until it was taken off road, shredding the ground in the process.

SPECIFICATIONS

ENGINE CAPACITY: 659 cc turbo
CONFIGURATION: front-mounted three-cylinder petrol
POWER: 47 kW (63 bhp)
TOP SPEED: n/a
TRANSMISSION: four-wheel drive
LENGTH: 3395 mm (133.66 in)
WIDTH: 1475 mm (58.07 in)
DEBUT: Geneva 2004

In a bid to capture the freedom of a motorcycle, the D-Bone's frame was exposed, along with its wheels.

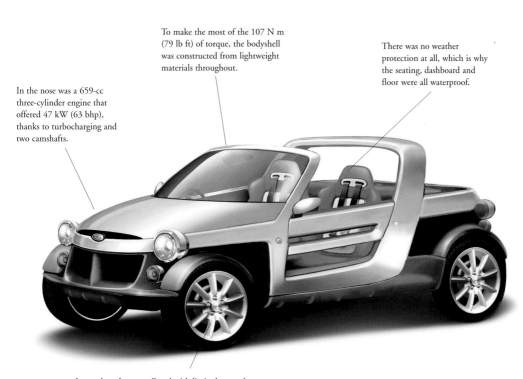

To make the most of the 107 N m (79 lb ft) of torque, the bodyshell was constructed from lightweight materials throughout.

There was no weather protection at all, which is why the seating, dashboard and floor were all waterproof.

In the nose was a 659-cc three-cylinder engine that offered 47 kW (63 bhp), thanks to turbocharging and two camshafts.

It may have been small and with limited ground clearance, but four-wheel drive enabled the car to go off-roading.

DODGE ESX3

W̶ith the Americans rarely being accused of building environmentally friendly cars, the ESX3 was Dodge's attempt at changing that. As the name suggested, the ESX3 was the third in a series of concepts that aimed to eke as many miles out of each gallon of fuel as possible. While the target was 80 miles (129 km) to each gallon (3.79 litres) of diesel, the ESX3 could manage 72 mpg (31 km/litre) – which was pretty good going for a five-seater saloon. This was achieved by reducing the car's weight to a minimum, while also incorporating cutting-edge technology under the skin – in the shape of a diesel/electric hybrid powertrain.

SPECIFICATIONS

ENGINE CAPACITY:	1.5-litre engine plus electric motor
CONFIGURATION:	front-mounted in-line four-cylinder diesel; rear-mounted electric motor
POWER:	55 kW (74 bhp) (diesel) plus 15 kW (20 bhp) (electric)
TOP SPEED:	n/a
TRANSMISSION:	automatic
LENGTH:	4897 mm (192.79 in)
WIDTH:	1885 mm (74.21 in)
DEBUT:	Geneva 2000

The taillights on the ESX3 gave a three-dimensional effect which was inspired by the fins of Chrylser's cars from the 1950s.

Although the company used plenty of advanced materials in the ESX3, Dodge claimed that 80 per cent of the vehicle could be recycled.

Up front there was a 1.5-litre diesel engine, assisted by an electric motor complete with regenerative braking.

Dodge gave the ESX3's sheared surfaces and faceted angles a name; it was termed 'faceted design'.

A plastic bodyshell helped to keep the weight down to just over a ton, helping the ESX3 to make the most of the 70 kW (94 bhp) available.

FIAT DOWNTOWN

There was never any chance of the Downtown emerging from any of Fiat's factories, but it did show what Fiat was capable of when it came to innovative city cars. Small cars are what Fiat is best at; icons such as the Topolino and 500 sum up all that's best about the Italian company. But these cars were conventionally engineered, while the Downtown was an electric vehicle – and those have never stood any chance of selling in significant numbers. With recyclable materials used throughout the Downtown and renewable energy used to power it, this was Fiat's attempt at saving the planet – but it came to nothing.

SPECIFICATIONS

ENGINE CAPACITY:	electric
CONFIGURATION:	rear-mounted battery pack and motors
POWER:	n/a
TOP SPEED:	100 km/h (62 mph)
TRANSMISSION:	rear-wheel drive
LENGTH:	2500 mm (98.43 in)
WIDTH:	1490 mm (58.66 in)
DEBUT:	Geneva 1993

Each rear wheel was driven by an electric motor, with the amount of power regulated by an electronic management system.

For the best possible visibility there was a lot of glass; the roof was also very high, to increase the interior space.

Despite the tiny proportions, there were three seats offered. These were arranged in a triangular formation with the two seats at the back.

Safety was important, too; besides a reinforced cage around the car's perimeter and door beams, there was an airbag for the driver.

A sodium sulphur battery pack offered a range of 190 km (118 miles) around town – or 300 km (186 miles) at a steady 50 km/h (31 mph).

FORD MODEL U

W hen your best-selling car to date is called the Model T, and you want to recall the good times, the obvious thing to do is pinch the name – or at least use something closely related. So it was with the Model U, which aimed to offer transport for the masses, just as the Model T had done getting on for a century before. But whereas the Model T had offered cheap, basic transport, the idea behind the Model U was that it would be a technological tour de force that used pioneering technology to solve some of the problems brought about by the car.

SPECIFICATIONS

ENGINE CAPACITY:	2.3-litre
CONFIGURATION:	front-mounted
POWER:	88 kW (118 bhp)
TOP SPEED:	n/a
TRANSMISSION:	hybrid electric
LENGTH:	4230 mm (166.54 in)
WIDTH:	1810 mm (71.26 in)
DEBUT:	Detroit 2003
DESIGNER:	Lauren van den Acker

The Model U featured the world's first hydrogen-fuelled internal combustion engine: a 2.3-litre supercharged four-cylinder unit.

An electric motor and a pair of clutches allowed power from the engine, the motor or both, depending on circumstances.

It was significant that this concept for the masses reflected the enormous rise in popularity of the off-roader.

To maximize efficiency there was a regenerative braking system. This reclaimed energy that would otherwise be lost during braking.

GHIA COCKPIT

I t's an unfortunate fact that cars with three wheels are seen as sadly lacking: inferior vehicles for those who can't afford any better. The reality of course is that a decently engineered three-wheeler with its single wheel at the back can be just as much fun as any car with a full complement of wheels. They can be rather cheaper to run as well, which is why Ghia's Cockpit was a wheel short; this was an economy car that was designed in the wake of the fuel-starved 1970s. Even now it looks modern, but it seems that four wheels will always rule where production cars are concerned.

SPECIFICATIONS

ENGINE CAPACITY:	200 cc
CONFIGURATION:	rear-mounted single-cylinder petrol
POWER:	9 kW (12 bhp)
TOP SPEED:	89 km/h (55 mph)
TRANSMISSION:	four-speed sequential, rear-wheel drive
LENGTH:	n/a
WIDTH:	n/a
DEBUT:	Geneva 1981

Access to the cabin was gained by lifting the canopy, which was hinged at the front and assisted by gas struts.

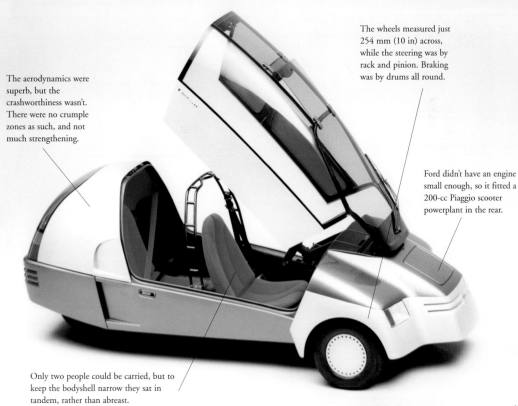

The aerodynamics were superb, but the crashworthiness wasn't. There were no crumple zones as such, and not much strengthening.

The wheels measured just 254 mm (10 in) across, while the steering was by rack and pinion. Braking was by drums all round.

Ford didn't have an engine small enough, so it fitted a 200-cc Piaggio scooter powerplant in the rear.

Only two people could be carried, but to keep the bodyshell narrow they sat in tandem, rather than abreast.

GM HY-WIRE

It may seem a bit obscure initially, but there's a big clue in the name of the GM Hy-Wire as to the technologies that it showcased – namely hydrogen fuel cell power and drive-by-wire electronics. Incorporating these two of the most important technologies to enter the automotive field at the start of the twenty-first century, the Hy-Wire was an evolution of GM's AUTO-nomy concept. It also showed that these new technologies could both be used in a practical, usable family car – even if there was no chance of the concept making it into production very soon after it made its debut at the 2003 Detroit motor show.

SPECIFICATIONS

ENGINE CAPACITY:	200 single fuel cells, connected in series
CONFIGURATION:	rear-mounted fuel stack
POWER:	129 kW (173 bhp)
TOP SPEED:	about 160 km/h (100 mph)
TRANSMISSION:	front-wheel drive
LENGTH:	4953 mm (195 in)
WIDTH:	1870 mm (73.62 in)
DEBUT:	Detroit 2003

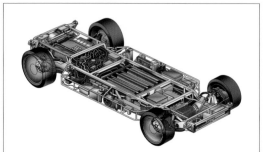

A hydrogen fuel cell provided the motive power – it also enabled an uncluttered cabin, along with a new method of car construction.

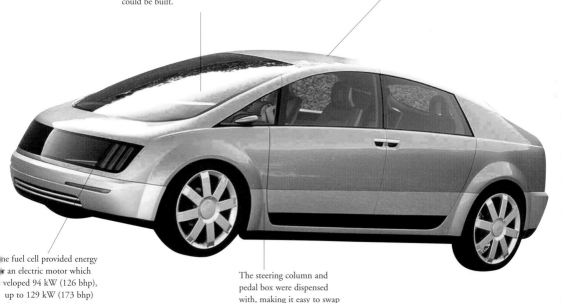

Perhaps the most important concept shown within the past two decades, the Hy-Wire shows how all mass-produced cars could be built.

One of the key technologies was the use of drive-by-wire. By eradicating mechanical linkages, the whole cabin could be opened up.

ne fuel cell provided energy
r an electric motor which
veloped 94 kW (126 bhp),
up to 129 kW (173 bhp)
short bursts.

The steering column and pedal box were dispensed with, making it easy to swap from left- to right-hand drive.

GM SEQUEL

First came the AUTO-nomy concept, then the Hy-Wire. The next step in GM's fuel-cell evolution was the Sequel, which the company claimed was the nearest thing to a production-ready vehicle to use such motive power. However, while most of the packaging issues had been resolved, there was still a major problem with building the cars at a price that consumers could afford. Even if the company pitched the Sequel as an ultra-luxurious premium SUV, GM would not have been able to make money on it or anything like it. But that wasn't to say that a solution couldn't be found – it just wasn't around the next corner.

SPECIFICATIONS

ENGINE CAPACITY:	fuel cell
CONFIGURATION:	front-mounted fuel-cell stack
POWER:	110 kW (148 bhp)
TOP SPEED:	145 km/h (90 mph)
TRANSMISSION:	CVT, four-wheel drive
LENGTH:	4994 mm (196.61 in)
WIDTH:	1966 mm (77.40 in)
DEBUT:	Detroit 2005

The car was powered by hydrogen, with three storage tanks located in the middle of the car underneath the passenger compartment.

There was a single electric motor for the front wheels, while each rear wheel was fitted with its own motor to give four-wheel drive.

As with the Hy-Wire, there was a platform that contained all the mechanicals. This was possible thanks to the use of drive-by-wire.

The Sequel was comparable in size to a full-sized SUV, and it was just as well equipped, too, with an ultra-luxurious cabin.

The Sequel's drivetrain was amazingly compact, with the fuel cell stack at the front and lithium ion batteries at the rear.

HAWTAL WHITING CONCEPT 92

Think about the all-time great design houses and it's unlikely that Hawtal Whiting would figure in the top 100, never mind the top 10. While few people have heard of this British design and engineering consultancy, it nonetheless has had a big hand in shaping some of Europe's biggest-selling cars. Unfortunately for Hawtal Whiting, the Concept 92 didn't go on to become one of them, although it was a good attempt at providing a solution to the buyers of small passenger and light commercial vehicles everywhere. Perhaps the company would have been more successful in the twenty-first century, thanks to the Concept 92's friendliness to the environment.

SPECIFICATIONS

ENGINE CAPACITY:	electric
CONFIGURATION:	front-mounted motor
POWER:	n/a
TOP SPEED:	n/a
TRANSMISSION:	front-wheel drive
LENGTH:	3050 mm (120.08 in)
WIDTH:	1740 mm (68.50 in)
DEBUT:	Autotech 1992

As well as the van version of Hawtal's Concept 92, there was a cabriolet and a five-seater people-carrier, with a high roof and plenty of glass.

Although the Concept 92 was not a wide vehicle, there was room for three people to sit abreast in the van.

The people-carrier featured front seats that swivelled by up to 45 degrees, to make entry and exit easier.

The Concept 92 was just three metres (10 ft) long – which was the same length as the iconic Issigonis-designed original Mini.

Although the concepts weren't runners, petrol and diesel power would have been offered, but electricity was favoured.

HONDA DUALNOTE

How would you like a car that offers nearly 298 kW (400 bhp) yet can still travel more than 80 km (50 miles) on a gallon of fuel? It's a tempting prospect, and one that Honda offered in the Dualnote that was first shown at the 2001 Tokyo motor show. But despite the fact that the car looked very futuristic, and some of the technology that it packed also appeared to be similarly unattainable, the reality was that everything under the skin of the Dualnote was possible to put into production there and then. It was just that it would have proved to be far too expensive for the average family to afford.

SPECIFICATIONS

ENGINE CAPACITY:	3.5-litre
CONFIGURATION:	mid-mounted V6, petrol
POWER:	294 kW (394 bhp)
TOP SPEED:	n/a
TRANSMISSION:	six-speed manual, rear-wheel drive
LENGTH:	4385 mm (172.64 in)
WIDTH:	1725 mm (67.91 in)
DEBUT:	Tokyo 2001

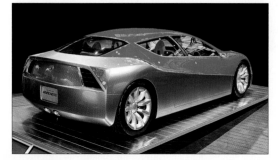

A 3.5-litre V6 petrol engine was positioned behind the rear-seat passengers, which helped to produce exceptional handling for the class of car.

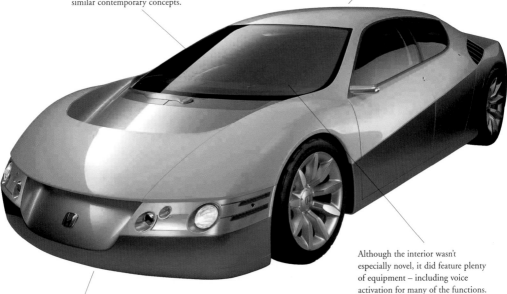

Looking more like a two-door coupé than the four-door hatch it was, this wasn't as pretty as other similar contemporary concepts.

Helping the petrol engine were three electric motors – by the time it was all added up there was 294 kW (394 bhp) available.

Although the interior wasn't especially novel, it did feature plenty of equipment – including voice activation for many of the functions.

There was four-wheel drive along with a six-speed clutchless manual gearbox that also featured a fully automatic mode.

HYUNDAI PORTICO

Once again Hyundai proved that it could come up with some great styling details – if not a beautiful overall design – while churning out unimaginative production cars by the thousand. However, unlike its HCD concepts, the Portico was designed in South Korea – and it showed. While the American studio generally produced covetable concepts, the Korean counterpart struggled to understand American and European tastes. This was still a good effort, though, with some clever technology incorporated into a bodyshell that was rather bland and unassuming. That's apart from the grille of course, which is astonishingly kitsch and one of those details that's likely to provoke nightmares.

SPECIFICATIONS

ENGINE CAPACITY:	2000 cc
CONFIGURATION:	front-mounted petrol V6
POWER:	112 kW (150 bhp)
TOP SPEED:	n/a
TRANSMISSION:	six-speed semi-auto, four-wheel drive
LENGTH:	5000 mm (196.85 in)
WIDTH:	2000 mm (78.74 in)
DEBUT:	Geneva 2005

By opting for two rows of three seats, up to six people could be carried, yet there was still space for luggage at the back.

The whole of the roof was made of glass, but to stop the occupants from cooking it could be instantly darkened with liquid crystal.

This was a cross between a saloon car and an MPV, with the driveability of the former and flexibility of the latter.

As was common by this time, the back doors were rear-hinged and there was no central pillar, to aid access to the interior.

The all-alloy V6 drove the front wheels, but electric motors could also drive all four wheels in hybrid mode.

MITSUBISHI CONCEPT-EZ MIEV

With the catchy name of Concept-EZ MIEV, it was very easy to overlook this show car from Mitsubishi – yet the technology it incorporated was much more far-reaching than at first appeared. It's that acronym MIEV that's the key, as it was short for Mitsubishi In-wheel Electric motor Vehicle. In other words, there was no bulky engine or other powerplant in the car's nose, and there was no conventional transmission either. Instead there were electric motors fitted to each wheel, which did away with driveshafts and a differential, freeing up passenger space and reducing weight. This car really did represent the future of car design.

SPECIFICATIONS

ENGINE CAPACITY:	electric
CONFIGURATION:	under-floor batteries, wheel-mounted motors
POWER:	82 kW (110 bhp)
TOP SPEED:	151 km/h (94 mph)
TRANSMISSION:	automatic, part-time four-wheel drive
LENGTH:	3700 mm (145.67 in)
WIDTH:	1800 mm (70.87 in)
DEBUT:	Geneva 2006

The seating could be configured in all sorts of ways, with the opportunity to carry people or luggage in any combination.

Despite such diminutive proportions, there was masses of interior space thanks to the clever engineering underneath.

Adopting a long wheelbase and keeping overhangs to a minimum opened up interior space even further.

There was also drive-by-wire, which did away with linkages for the steering and brakes; the transmission was automatic.

Although functionality was the name of the game, Mitsubishi couldn't resist fitting 508-mm (20-in) wheels for some aggression.

79

NISSAN CYPACT

H aving fun while driving and being kind to the planet are normally mutually exclusive experiences, but, with the Cypact, Nissan aimed to change all that. This was to be a small car that offered fun and economy in equal doses, thanks to an ultra-efficient turbodiesel engine that incorporated the latest technology such as direct injection and a variable-nozzle turbocharger, along with common-rail fuel delivery. With a capacity of just 1.2 litres, the 56 kW (75 bhp) output was impressive, but not as much as the cleanliness and economy; 35 km/litre (83 mpg) was possible, along with CO_2 emissions of just 90g/km – 30 per cent better than was typical for the sector.

SPECIFICATIONS

ENGINE CAPACITY:	1.2 litres
CONFIGURATION:	front-engined turbodiesel four-cylinder
POWER:	56 kW (75 bhp)
TOP SPEED:	n/a
TRANSMISSION:	five-speed manual, front-wheel drive
LENGTH:	3740 mm (147.24 in)
WIDTH:	1630 mm (64.17 in)
DEBUT:	Frankfurt 1999

Despite offering up to 35 km/litre (83 mpg), there was space for four inside – yet the Cypact was barely any bigger than a Micra.

Until this point, all diesel engines had been made of cast iron. The Cypact introduced the lightweight all-alloy diesel engine.

To help maximize interior space there was an unusually high roofline, while the doors were oversized for easy access.

The interior was cheerful and inviting, with a blue-and-white colour scheme and thinly padded seats to increase space.

As well as air conditioning, there was a multimedia system that linked satellite navigation with real-time travel information.

NISSAN YANYA

Whence two seemingly opposing sectors of the market take off, there's a school of thought that says that, if you combine the two in one car, you can't help but take customers from each segment. So when the global market saw rises in supermini and SUV sales in the early twenty-first century, Nissan decided that by putting the two sectors together it could create a new kind of car – the off-roading supermini. But just in case two sectors wasn't enough, Nissan threw in a third and fourth – because the Yanya was capable of being turned into a full convertible or even a pick-up truck!

SPECIFICATIONS

ENGINE CAPACITY:	n/a
CONFIGURATION:	front-mounted petrol
POWER:	n/a
TOP SPEED:	n/a
TRANSMISSION:	part-time four-wheel
LENGTH:	drive
	n/a
WIDTH:	n/a
DEBUT:	Geneva 2002

*The Yanya combined the characteristics
of an SUV with those of a city car, a pick-up
and even a convertible.*

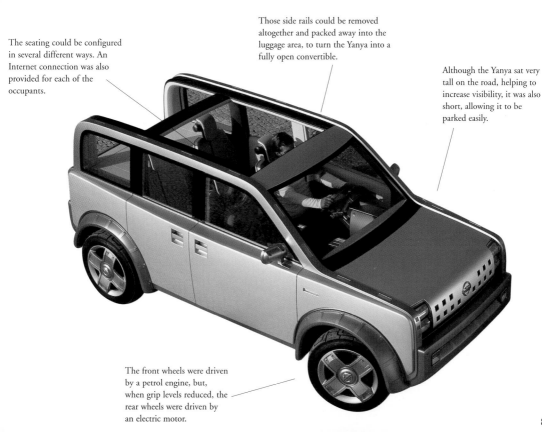

The seating could be configured in several different ways. An Internet connection was also provided for each of the occupants.

Those side rails could be removed altogether and packed away into the luggage area, to turn the Yanya into a fully open convertible.

Although the Yanya sat very tall on the road, helping to increase visibility, it was also short, allowing it to be parked easily.

The front wheels were driven by a petrol engine, but, when grip levels reduced, the rear wheels were driven by an electric motor.

83

OPEL JUNIOR

The aim of the Junior was to provide transport in comfort for up to four people, while occupying as little road space as possible – and at the same time also being cheap to run and fun to drive. That meant that not only did the car have to be as space efficient inside as possible, but it also had to sit rather taller than was usual for small cars at the time. Although cars have become taller to allow greater interior space without having to be significantly longer or wider, when the Junior was unveiled it was unusual – although far from unprecedented – to simply build upwards.

SPECIFICATIONS

ENGINE CAPACITY:	1.2 litres
CONFIGURATION:	front-mounted three-cylinder petrol
POWER:	41 kW (55 bhp)
TOP SPEED:	151 km/h (94 mph)
TRANSMISSION:	front-wheel drive
LENGTH:	3410 mm (134.25 in)
WIDTH:	1570 mm (61.81 in)
DEBUT:	Frankfurt 1983

The interior was ultra-practical with cubby holes everywhere and the bare minimum of instrumentation, which could be easily upgraded.

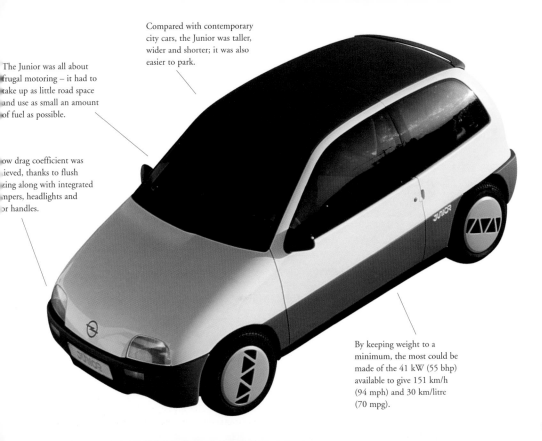

The Junior was all about frugal motoring – it had to take up as little road space and use as small an amount of fuel as possible.

ow drag coefficient was ieved, thanks to flush zing along with integrated npers, headlights and or handles.

Compared with contemporary city cars, the Junior was taller, wider and shorter; it was also easier to park.

By keeping weight to a minimum, the most could be made of the 41 kW (55 bhp) available to give 151 km/h (94 mph) and 30 km/litre (70 mpg).

OPEL MAXX

There were short- and long-wheelbase versions of the Maxx, powered by the then-new 973-cc cast-iron three-cylinder engine that would become the entry-level powerplant for the Corsa. In short-wheelbase form the Maxx was 750 mm (29.53 in) shorter than the Corsa; by using aluminium extensively in its construction, the fuel efficiency and manoeuvrability of the car were superb. The car was 75 mm (three inches) shorter than the original Mini, but despite its compact dimensions there were two rows of seats installed – giving enough space to house four people. Thanks to its slippery shape, the low rolling resistance of the tyres and the lightweight construction, the car could supposedly achieve 31 km/litre (72 mpg).

SPECIFICATIONS

ENGINE CAPACITY:	973 cc
CONFIGURATION:	front-mounted three-cylinder petrol
POWER:	37 kW (50 bhp)
TOP SPEED:	153 km/h (95 mph)
TRANSMISSION:	five-speed sequential, four-wheel drive
LENGTH:	2975 mm (117.13 in)
WIDTH:	1575 mm (62.01 in)
DEBUT:	Geneva 1995

The steeply sloped front end improved aerodynamics, while the rear was sharply cut off to maximize interior space.

ong and short versions of
he Maxx were built. They
ere both comparatively
mall, though, as they were
med at city drivers.

There were plenty of
lightweight materials such as
aluminium and plastic used,
to ensure the Maxx was as
frugal as possible.

The interior was simple with
not much gadgetry, as this
was an economy car, but
there was a telephone.

A three-cylinder 1-litre
engine gave plenty of
performance in town, while
a five-speed sequential/auto
gearbox made it easy to
drive.

PININFARINA ETHOS 3

The Ethos 3 was the third (and final) concept in a series of running prototypes developed by Pininfarina. As with the previous editions, the Ethos 3 took a look at how efficiently a small car could be packaged, while also toying with new construction methods. With a tall but narrow body, there was space for six people (in two rows of three), yet the car was just 3241 mm (127.60 in) long. While it was no beauty, the packaging was impressive. Its diminutive proportions meant the Ethos 3's weight could be kept right down, which allowed an Orbital two-stroke engine to offer both strong performance and low fuel consumption.

SPECIFICATIONS

ENGINE CAPACITY:	1197 cc
CONFIGURATION:	front-mounted in-line three-cylinder
POWER:	71 kW (95 bhp)
TOP SPEED:	n/a
TRANSMISSION:	continuously variable, front-wheel drive
LENGTH:	3241 mm (127.60 in)
WIDTH:	1689 mm (66.50 in)
DEBUT:	Turin 1994

Powering the Ethos 3 was a 1.2-litre two-stroke engine. With three cylinders and 71 kW (95 bhp), it was powerful but economical.

The body panels were all made of plastic, hung onto an extruded aluminium frame to keep weight down.

The steering wheel could be moved from one side of the car to the other – complete with the pedals and instruments.

Goodyear produced a set of low rolling resistance tyres, to improve fuel economy – also aided by a total weight of just 780 kg (1720 lb).

The front wheels were driven via a continuously variable transmission, ensuring the car would always be in the right gear.

RENAULT ZOOM

When you look at the Zoom it doesn't look as if many of the technologies it incorporated would be retained if it went into production. When the car was costed out, however, Renault claimed that, for the same sort of price as a mid-range Clio, the car could be built with composite bodywork and an adjustable wheelbase. These composite panels were self-coloured, so there was no need to paint the car, while the chassis, door structures and some of the suspension components were produced from recycled materials. Incredibly, the waistline of the Zoom's bodyshell featured self-healing paintwork for when the car was scratched.

SPECIFICATIONS

ENGINE CAPACITY:	electric
CONFIGURATION:	front-mounted, transverse
POWER:	25 kW (33 bhp)
TOP SPEED:	121 km/h (75 mph)
TRANSMISSION:	continuously variable transmission, front-wheel drive
LENGTH:	2650 mm (104.33 in)
WIDTH:	1520 mm (59.84 in)
DEBUT:	Paris 1992

The Zoom was powered by electricity – and, as nobody had overcome the shortcomings of this at the time, production was never a possibility.

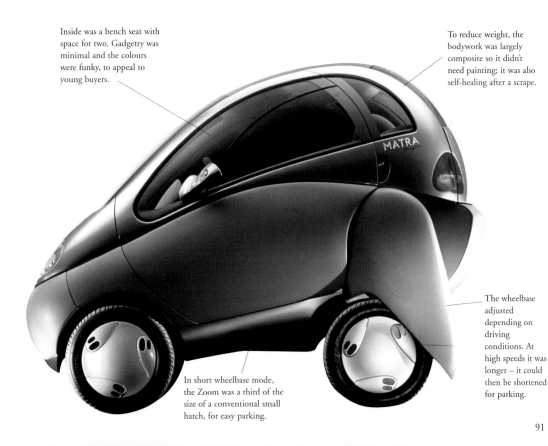

Inside was a bench seat with space for two. Gadgetry was minimal and the colours were funky, to appeal to young buyers.

To reduce weight, the bodywork was largely composite so it didn't need painting; it was also self-healing after a scrape.

MATRA

The wheelbase adjusted depending on driving conditions. At high speeds it was longer – it could then be shortened for parking.

In short wheelbase mode, the Zoom was a third of the size of a conventional small hatch, for easy parking.

91

RINSPEED SENSO

A nother strange idea from Frank Rinderknecht's Swiss company, the Senso was a car which detected its driver's biometric data and adjusted various elements to suit. So depending on the driver's pulse, blood pressure and alertness, the Senso could alter the colour of the interior lighting, play different types of music within the cabin and even emit different fragrances. As if this weren't mad enough, the Senso was also environmentally friendly, as it ran on natural gas. Or at least it was probably as environmentally friendly as it's possible to be when there is a Porsche Boxster 3.2-litre flat-six mounted in the middle.

SPECIFICATIONS

ENGINE CAPACITY:	3179 cc
CONFIGURATION:	flat-six petrol
POWER:	186 kW (250 bhp)
TOP SPEED:	250 km/h (155 mph)
TRANSMISSION:	six-speed manual, rear-wheel drive
LENGTH:	4475 mm (176.18 in)
WIDTH:	1820 mm (71.65 in)
DEBUT:	Geneva 2005

Sensors in the cabin could detect how often the driver changed lanes and how close to the car in front he or she was driving.

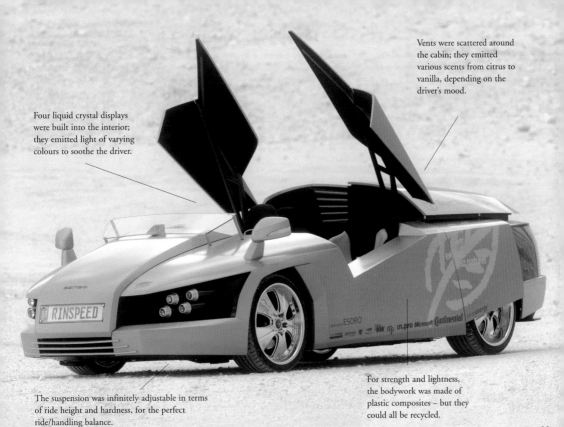

Four liquid crystal displays were built into the interior; they emitted light of varying colours to soothe the driver.

Vents were scattered around the cabin; they emitted various scents from citrus to vanilla, depending on the driver's mood.

The suspension was infinitely adjustable in terms of ride height and hardness, for the perfect ride/handling balance.

For strength and lightness, the bodywork was made of plastic composites – but they could all be recycled.

SMART CROSSTOWN

Smart has never had an easy life. The DaimlerChrysler sub-brand has struggled to sell enough of its expensively built cars to make the sums add up, and, having expanded then contracted the range in a bid to stem huge losses, the company attempted to move itself into a more profitable era with the Crosstown. By mixing funky lines with cutting-edge technology, Smart could finally justify the high prices that it was forced to ask for its products. As a result, the Crosstown used a petrol-electric hybrid drivetrain for maximum power and minimum fuel consumption. The question remained, though: could Smart make the sums add up?

SPECIFICATIONS

ENGINE CAPACITY:	698 cc
CONFIGURATION:	rear-mounted in-line three-cylinder petrol
POWER:	45 kW (60 bhp)
TOP SPEED:	135 km/h (84 mph)
TRANSMISSION:	six-speed semi-auto, rear-wheel drive
LENGTH:	2685 mm (105.71 in)
WIDTH:	1586 mm (62.44 in)
DEBUT:	Frankfurt 2005

The Crosstown was first displayed in metallic green; at the Geneva 2005 show the vehicle emerged with a matt grey finish.

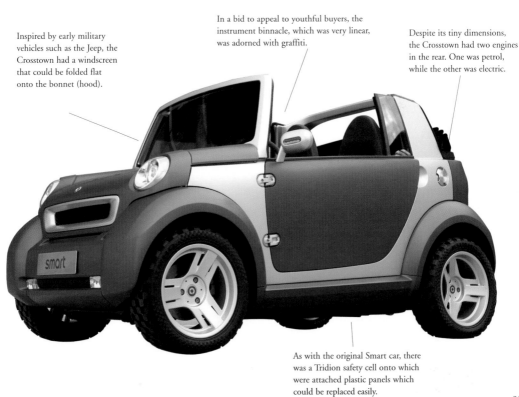

Inspired by early military vehicles such as the Jeep, the Crosstown had a windscreen that could be folded flat onto the bonnet (hood).

In a bid to appeal to youthful buyers, the instrument binnacle, which was very linear, was adorned with graffiti.

Despite its tiny dimensions, the Crosstown had two engines in the rear. One was petrol, while the other was electric.

As with the original Smart car, there was a Tridion safety cell onto which were attached plastic panels which could be replaced easily.

SUBARU B9 SCRAMBLER

Subaru had tried sports cars before, but these had always been coupés rather than roadsters. For a first attempt at an open-topped two-seater, the B9 Scrambler was a pretty good effort, even if the nose was a little fussy and the interior was somewhat overdesigned. While the lines were generally very pleasing, however, it was the technology underneath that mattered. As well as a flat-four petrol engine in the nose, there was a hybrid drivetrain that allowed the car to be driven on electricity, with the batteries charged through regenerative braking. Even better, it's technology that's now becoming commonplace in production cars.

SPECIFICATIONS

ENGINE CAPACITY:	1994 cc
CONFIGURATION:	front-mounted flat-four, petrol
POWER:	104 kW (140 bhp)
TOP SPEED:	n/a
TRANSMISSION:	four-wheel drive
LENGTH:	4200 mm (165.35 in)
WIDTH:	1880 mm (74.02 in)
DEBUT:	Geneva 2004

Instead of the usual nickel-hydride batteries, on the B9 Scrambler there were manganese-lithium-ion units which were more efficient and reliable.

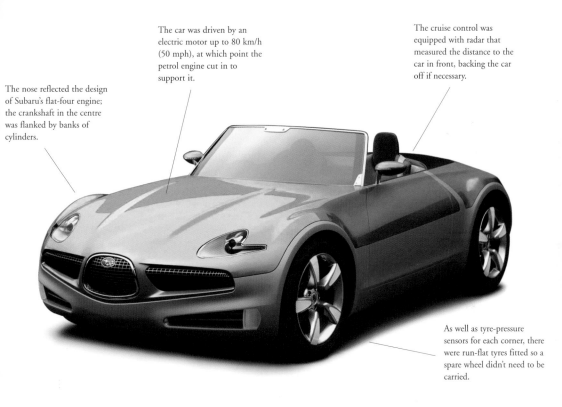

The nose reflected the design of Subaru's flat-four engine; the crankshaft in the centre was flanked by banks of cylinders.

The car was driven by an electric motor up to 80 km/h (50 mph), at which point the petrol engine cut in to support it.

The cruise control was equipped with radar that measured the distance to the car in front, backing the car off if necessary.

As well as tyre-pressure sensors for each corner, there were run-flat tyres fitted so a spare wheel didn't need to be carried.

TOYOTA ALESSANDRO VOLTA

Styled by Italian styling house Italdesign, but carrying the Toyota badge, the Alessandro Volta was a hybrid supercar that aimed to offer 250 km/h (155 mph) performance, but with the fuel economy of a family car. Using the mechanicals of the Lexus RX400h off-roader, the Alessandro Volta was named after the Italian physicist who discovered the voltaic pile – not that many people would have realized it. Although neither Toyota nor Italdesign had made much of it before, this concept followed a quarter of a century of collaborations between the two companies. Sadly, though, there was never any chance of this car making production, as Lexus was already working on its own supercar.

SPECIFICATIONS

ENGINE CAPACITY:	3.3-litre
CONFIGURATION:	mid-mounted petrol V6/electric hybrid
POWER:	300 kW (402 bhp)
TOP SPEED:	250 km/h (155 mph)
TRANSMISSION:	four-wheel drive
LENGTH:	4358 mm (171.57 in)
WIDTH:	1925 mm (75.79 in)
DEBUT:	Geneva 2004

In true supercar fashion, the Alessandro Volta had doors that were hinged to open upwards rather than outwards. Italdesign termed this 'dragonfly-style'.

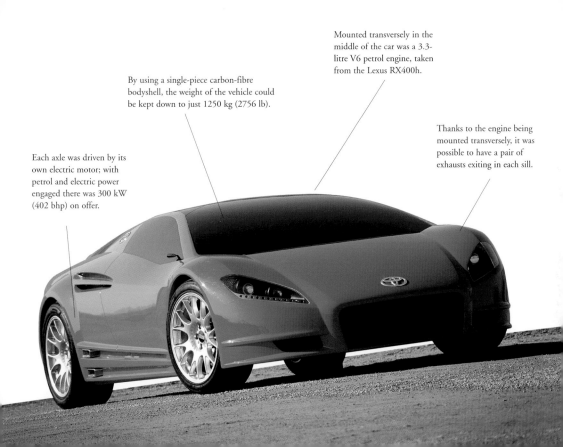

Mounted transversely in the middle of the car was a 3.3-litre V6 petrol engine, taken from the Lexus RX400h.

By using a single-piece carbon-fibre bodyshell, the weight of the vehicle could be kept down to just 1250 kg (2756 lb).

Thanks to the engine being mounted transversely, it was possible to have a pair of exhausts exiting in each sill.

Each axle was driven by its own electric motor; with petrol and electric power engaged there was 300 kW (402 bhp) on offer.

VOLKSWAGEN ECORACER

Maximum fun with minimum fuel consumption was the key to VW's EcoRacer. That's why this was a sports car that packed a diesel engine while also taking up the minimum of road space. Although the car was billed as a research vehicle, it revealed some of the ideas that would hopefully make it into some of Volkswagen's production cars. One thing that would reach showrooms was the all-new 1.5-litre turbodiesel engine which sat in the middle of the car. With 249 N m (184 lb ft) of torque, it endowed the EcoRacer with a very healthy power to weight ratio of 119 kW (160 bhp) per ton.

SPECIFICATIONS

ENGINE CAPACITY:	1484 cc
CONFIGURATION:	mid-mounted in-line four-cylinder turbodiesel
POWER:	101 kW (136 bhp)
TOP SPEED:	230 km/h (143 mph)
TRANSMISSION:	semi-auto, rear-wheel drive
LENGTH:	3765 mm (148.23 in)
WIDTH:	1738 mm (68.43 in)
DEBUT:	Tokyo 2005

With an ultra-light carbon-fibre monocoque, the EcoRacer's handling was amazingly sharp, while fuel economy was superb.

There were just two seats on offer, with the small turbodiesel engine sitting behind the simply trimmed cabin.

For the maximum possible agility, the EcoRacer was both short and narrow, with very short overhangs at each end.

The interior was like a racing car's, with thinly padded seats, a small steering wheel, cast aluminium controls and carbon-fibre trim.

For a concept car, those wheels were surprisingly restrained. They measured 432 mm (17 in) across and carried Bridgestone Potenza tyres.

PRODUCTION REALITIES

Not all show cars end their days languishing in warehouses; sometimes they make it into production. And the good news is that this is becoming an ever more common occurrence. The downside is that many concepts are now little more than thinly disguised early debuts for showroom-ready vehicles. Also, many of the concepts that do make it to the showrooms are watered down so much that it's hard to see the similarities between the two. For example, take a look at the Citroën Xanae and Land Rover Range Stormer and you may struggle to see how they became the Xsara Picasso and Range Rover Sport, respectively.

This chapter contains some of the concepts that went all the way – or at least were seriously considered for production. Sadly, that means it also contains cars that came close to production, but were canned for whatever reason – fabulous designs such as the Jaguar F-Type and Lamborghini Miura that really should have made it. At the time of writing, some of the models had yet to appear in the showrooms, but, if vehicles such as the Fiat Trepiuno and Aston Martin Rapide should fail to materialize, those would surely be some of the most disappointing wasted opportunities in the short history of the car.

Left: *One of the most successful concept car designs ever, the Audi TT hardly changed from exhibition hall to showroom.*

ALFA ROMEO PROTEO

When the Alfa Romeo-based 164 Proteo was unveiled at the 1991 Geneva motor show, it was announced that there would be 2000 examples available. To prove that Alfa Romeo was serious, three running prototypes were constructed, but the company got cold feet within weeks of the car's debut and the project was axed. The Proteo was intended to be a small, technologically advanced premium sports car. With a 3-litre V6 engine that drove all four wheels, there was also four-wheel steering, which was briefly all the rage around this time – but it seems the project was simply too daring for Alfa, and the Proteo was canned.

SPECIFICATIONS

ENGINE CAPACITY:	2959 cc
CONFIGURATION:	front-mounted V6, petrol
POWER:	194 kW (260 bhp)
TOP SPEED:	250 km/h (155 mph)
TRANSMISSION:	five-speed manual
LENGTH:	4155 mm (163.58 in)
WIDTH:	1812 mm (71.34 in)
DEBUT:	Geneva 1991
DESIGNER:	Walter de Silva

The Alfa Romeo Proteo was based on a cut-down Alfa Romeo 164 3.0 V6 platform, with the addition of four-wheel drive.

The glass was coated to reduce heat build-up inside. Named Solextra, it reduced interior temperatures by 42 per cent.

In keeping with the sporting image, there would be only a five-speed manual transmission, as fitted to the 164.

All four wheels were steered, to give greater manoeuvrability at low speeds and more stability when moving faster.

Those 432-mm (17-in) alloy wheels wrapped in low-profile 235/45 ZR17 rubber were unusual at the time. They soon became popular, though.

ASTON MARTIN RAPIDE

With Porsche announcing its Panamera four-door saloon, Aston Martin was galvanized into action a few months before the 2006 Detroit motor show, where the Rapide made its debut. While the nose was pure DB9, the profile was an altogether different beast, with those muscular haunches that swept all the way through to the back. The roofline was ultra-low, which limited interior space to a degree, but seats set very low made up for this. Mechanically the Rapide was the same as the DB9, but with more power and stronger brakes. One of the many high points was the fabulous interior, with wood, alloy and grained leather everywhere.

SPECIFICATIONS

ENGINE CAPACITY:	5935 cc
CONFIGURATION:	front-engined V12
POWER:	358 kW (480 bhp)
TOP SPEED:	290 km/h (180 mph) plus
TRANSMISSION:	six-speed semi-auto
LENGTH:	5000 mm (196.85 in)
WIDTH:	1866 mm (73.46 in)
DEBUT:	Detroit 2006
DESIGNER:	Marek Reichman

This wasn't the first time Aston Martin had produced a four-door saloon, but the Rapide was easily the best-looking.

The whole of the roof was a polycarbonate panel which incorporated liquid crystal; it could be darkened at the flick of a switch.

Although the engine was taken from the DB9, it was boosted to 358 kW (480 bhp); this was mated to a semiautomatic transmission.

The wheelbase was extended by 25 cm (10 in) over the DB9; Aston Martin's 'VH' alloy platform was designed with this flexibility in mind.

This was the first time Aston Martin had experimented with carbon brakes, which rival manufacturers had already embraced.

AUDI TT

It's unheard of for a concept car to make it into production in unchanged form – but the Audi TT must rank as one of the least interfered with designs ever. While the rear pillar treatment had to be modified substantially to allow the driver to see out, the rest of the lines were barely touched in the transition from show to showroom. Look at the rest of the design – including the interior – and you'll be equally hard-pressed to spot many significant differences. At first there was just the TT coupé concept, but at the 1995 Tokyo motor show the TTS roadster made its debut – which also went into production.

SPECIFICATIONS

ENGINE CAPACITY:	1781 cc
CONFIGURATION:	front-mounted in-line four petrol
POWER:	112 kW (150 bhp)
TOP SPEED:	225 km/h (140 mph)
TRANSMISSION:	five-speed manual, front-wheel drive
LENGTH:	4002 mm (157.56 in)
WIDTH:	1751 mm (68.94 in)
DEBUT:	Frankfurt 1995
DESIGNER:	Romulus Rost

Although production cars would use Audi's quattro four-wheel drive system, the TT concept used VW's Syncro set-up.

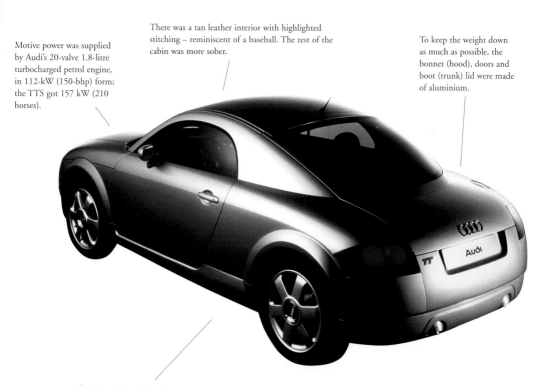

Motive power was supplied by Audi's 20-valve 1.8-litre turbocharged petrol engine, in 112-kW (150-bhp) form; the TTS got 157 kW (210 horses).

There was a tan leather interior with highlighted stitching – reminiscent of a baseball. The rest of the cabin was more sober.

To keep the weight down as much as possible, the bonnet (hood), doors and boot (trunk) lid were made of aluminium.

The TT could be built affordably by basing it on the Volkswagen Golf's floorpan, complete with all its running gear.

BMW Z9 TURISMO

The Z9 Gran Turismo burst onto the scene at the 1999 Frankfurt motor show; it was one of the first BMWs to lose the elegant and graceful look for something more controversial. With an aggressive nose that offered a total rethink of the BMW corporate grille, there were also sculpted headlights and a deep air dam for an air of sportiness. At first glance the Z9 looks like the work of BMW's controversial then head of design Chris Bangle, but it was Adrian van Hooydonk, one of the company's in-house designers, who penned it. Crucially, while the car looked radical as the Z9, it later entered production as the 6-Series.

SPECIFICATIONS

ENGINE CAPACITY:	3901 cc turbocharged
CONFIGURATION:	front-mounted V8 diesel
POWER:	180 kW (241 bhp)
TOP SPEED:	250 km/h (155 mph) (limited)
TRANSMISSION:	five-speed semiauto, rear-wheel drive
LENGTH:	4840 mm (190.55 in)
WIDTH:	1950 mm (76.77 in)
DEBUT:	Frankfurt 1999
DESIGNER:	Adrian van Hooydonk

The Z9 was powered by diesel, to dispel the myth that petrol is the only possible source of fuel for a sports car.

The interior featured BMW's I-Drive system to control many of the major functions. A steering column-mounted lever changed gears.

Another misconception dispelled was that of a grand touring car having to be heavy; aluminium and carbon fibre kept the weight down.

The Z9 brought a new nose treatment that would be used on production cars. Initially few liked it, but it has become more accepted.

Although the Z9 introduced a new BMW look, familiar styling cues such as the kinked C-pillar and prominent swage line remained.

CADILLAC EVOQ

With its buyers getting ever older, Cadillac needed to appeal to a younger market – and fast. The result was a new design direction typified by the Evoq, with sharp lines and a lack of fussy details. There was also some genuinely innovative technology in there, in a bid to appeal to gadget-conscious young buyers who wanted to stand out from the crowd. While not all of the technology installed in the Evoq has yet made it into production, at least the car itself has reached the showrooms in barely altered form. Slightly later than promised, the XLR went on sale in 2003.

SPECIFICATIONS

ENGINE CAPACITY:	4228 cc supercharged
CONFIGURATION:	front-mounted V8, petrol
POWER:	302 kW (405 bhp)
TOP SPEED:	250 km/h (155 mph)
TRANSMISSION:	four-speed automatic, rear-wheel drive
LENGTH:	4282 mm (168.58 in)
WIDTH:	1834 mm (72.20 in)
DEBUT:	Detroit 1999
DESIGNER:	Kip Wasenko

Although it initially looked like a coupé, the Evoq was actually a convertible, with a folding metal hard top to increase refinement and security.

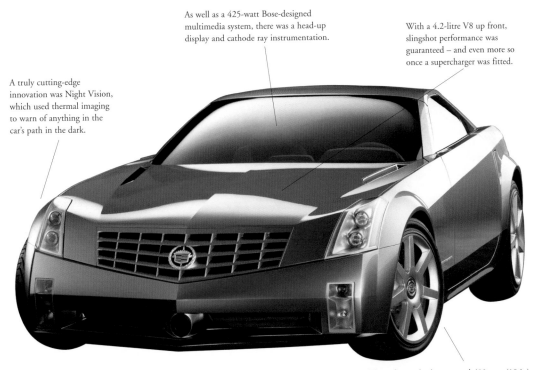

As well as a 425-watt Bose-designed multimedia system, there was a head-up display and cathode ray instrumentation.

With a 4.2-litre V8 up front, slingshot performance was guaranteed – and even more so once a supercharger was fitted.

A truly cutting-edge innovation was Night Vision, which used thermal imaging to warn of anything in the car's path in the dark.

Those front wheels measured 483 mm (19 in) across – the rear items were two inches bigger. They were wrapped in run-flat tyres.

113

CHEVROLET CAMARO

Heritage was the name of the game when it came to America's Big Three in the early part of the twenty-first century – and specifically the cynical cashing in on it. Ford had shown its Mustang and Thunderbird concepts, while DaimlerChrysler showed its Challenger show car. General Motors didn't want to be left behind, which is why it unveiled its backward-looking Camaro at the 2006 Detroit motor show. To be fair, the car looked fantastic, but it was still nothing more than a rehashed 40-year-old design. Still, if Ford could pull the trick off of repackaging a car from the 1960s for production, why shouldn't the General give it a go?

SPECIFICATIONS

ENGINE CAPACITY:	6 litres
CONFIGURATION:	front-mounted petrol V8
POWER:	298 kW (400 bhp)
TOP SPEED:	n/a
TRANSMISSION:	six-speed manual, rear-wheel drive
LENGTH:	4730 mm (186.22 in)
WIDTH:	2022 mm (79.61 in)
DEBUT:	Detroit 2006

The transmission was thoroughly modern, as it featured six ratios and was controlled by the driver rather than electronics.

That long bonnet (hood), short rear deck and ultra-wide bodyshell were classic muscle-car design cues that bristled with aggression.

The Camaro wasn't all show and no go – there was a 6-litre V8 engine at the front that could develop up to 298 kW (400 bhp).

Officially there was room for four, but the reality was that only those in the front would be able to have legs.

Even though the engine was big and powerful, it could deactivate half of its cylinders to give better fuel economy.

CHEVROLET SSR

Chrysler had enjoyed a certain amount of success with its PT Cruiser, with its lines harking back to the 1940s. With the gamble having paid off, Chevrolet decided that it, too, could produce a modern-day car that looked as though it had been put together six decades previously. The SSR, or Super Sports Roadster, was the result, and it combined the exhilaration of a convertible with the practicality of a pick-up – although this latter trait was somewhat compromised by the retractable roof that stowed in the load bay. Two years after the initial debut a production-ready SSR was shown, and within months it was on sale – complete with the retractable hard top.

SPECIFICATIONS

ENGINE CAPACITY:	6 litres
CONFIGURATION:	front-mounted petrol V8
POWER:	224 kW (300 bhp)
TOP SPEED:	n/a
TRANSMISSION:	four-speed auto, rear-wheel drive
LENGTH:	4727 mm (186.10 in)
WIDTH:	1997 mm (78.62 in)
DEBUT:	Detroit 2000

There was only one powerplant that could be fitted to a big American bruiser such as the SSR, and that was a V8 – in 6-litre form.

Strictly speaking there was really room for only two, but a third person could be squeezed onto the bench seat.

Perhaps the neatest aspect was the retractable hard top, which could be stowed vertically between the seat and the storage bed.

CHEVROLET

Those massively flared wheelarches were one of the key styling elements borrowed from Chevrolets of the 1940s.

Like any concept car worth its salt, there were massive alloy wheels fitted. The rears were 508 mm (20 in) across, the fronts 25 mm (an inch) less.

CITROËN C6 LIGNAGE

Where Citroën had once stood for innovation and timeless elegance, by the end of the twentieth century the company's products had become derivative and predictable. That's why a return to Citroën's core values was essential if it was to stand out from the crowd once more. The result was the C6 Lignage, which later went into production as the C6. While French luxury cars have never been successful in sales terms, this concept was created to show that Citroën could still innovate; a head-up display was fitted, along with swivelling headlights and an intelligent speed-regulation system which helped to avoid collisions, thanks to integrated obstacle detection.

SPECIFICATIONS

ENGINE CAPACITY:	n/a
CONFIGURATION:	front-mounted
POWER:	n/a
TOP SPEED:	n/a
TRANSMISSION:	front-wheel drive
LENGTH:	4920 mm (193.70 in)
WIDTH:	1890 mm (74.41 in)
DEBUT:	Geneva 1999
DESIGNER:	Mark Lloyd

The interior was designed to feel especially spacious, which is why the materials chosen were all lightly coloured.

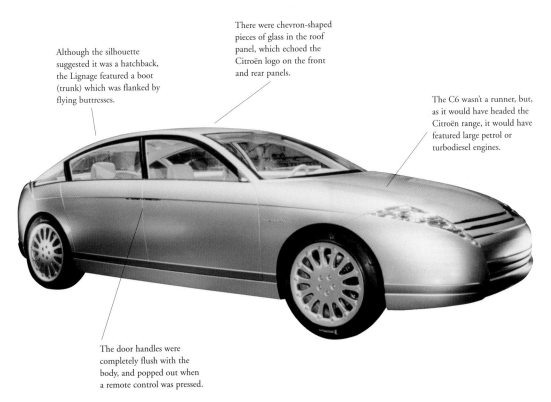

Although the silhouette suggested it was a hatchback, the Lignage featured a boot (trunk) which was flanked by flying buttresses.

There were chevron-shaped pieces of glass in the roof panel, which echoed the Citroën logo on the front and rear panels.

The C6 wasn't a runner, but, as it would have headed the Citroën range, it would have featured large petrol or turbodiesel engines.

The door handles were completely flush with the body, and popped out when a remote control was pressed.

CITROËN XANAE

In hindsight it's not hard to see that this is the concept that ultimately became the Xsara Picasso, but when it was first shown at the 1994 Paris motor show the Xanae looked highly innovative. Taking the idea of a full-sized MPV such as the Renault Espace, but shrinking it down into a more manageable package, the Xanae introduced the idea of a mid-sized people-carrier that offered much more space and comfort than a conventional saloon, but took up barely any more road space. Even better, while some of the detailing disappeared in the transition to production car, the basic idea of the Xanae didn't change at all.

SPECIFICATIONS

ENGINE CAPACITY:	1998 cc
CONFIGURATION:	front-mounted in-line four-cylinder
POWER:	112 kW (150 bhp)
TOP SPEED:	n/a
TRANSMISSION:	five-speed automatic, front-wheel drive
LENGTH:	4230 mm (166.54 in)
WIDTH:	1800 mm (70.87 in)
DEBUT:	Paris 1994
DESIGNER:	Mark Lloyd Marc Pinson

To open up the cabin of the Xanae as much as possible, there was plenty of glass, including a roof that was partly glazed.

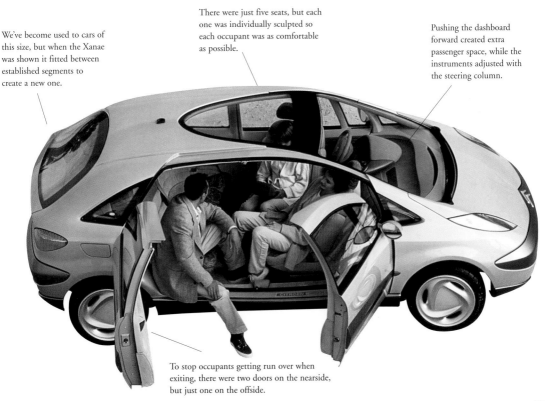

We've become used to cars of this size, but when the Xanae was shown it fitted between established segments to create a new one.

There were just five seats, but each one was individually sculpted so each occupant was as comfortable as possible.

Pushing the dashboard forward created extra passenger space, while the instruments adjusted with the steering column.

To stop occupants getting run over when exiting, there were two doors on the nearside, but just one on the offside.

DODGE VIPER

The car had been around for more than a century when the Viper made its debut, and with 100 years of development the fastest of sports cars were getting rather sanitized. An antidote was needed, and the Viper was it. This would be a car with huge reserves of power and torque, yet there would be no electronic aids to keep the driver out of trouble. Weight would be kept to a minimum by omitting pieces of equipment that everyone else was fitting as standard, and there would be the most dramatic styling imaginable. But the best bit? The car went into production in this form!

SPECIFICATIONS

ENGINE CAPACITY:	8 litres
CONFIGURATION:	front-mounted V10, petrol
POWER:	224 kW (300 bhp)
TOP SPEED:	233 km/h (145 mph)
TRANSMISSION:	five-speed manual, rear-wheel drive
LENGTH:	4448 mm (175.12 in)
WIDTH:	1923 mm (75.71 in)
DEBUT:	Detroit 1989

The exterior styling of the Viper was very clean – Dodge resisted the temptation to go overboard with scoops, slats and spoilers.

Although there were no electronic aids to help the driver, there was all-independent suspension and disc brakes all round.

The interior was as basic as the chassis; there was no air conditioning, electric windows or central locking, to keep weight down.

As if the Viper didn't look menacing enough, the exhaust pipes exited from the side of the car, in true hot-rod style.

The 8-litre V10 mounted up front was essentially a truck engine – which is why it was massively torquey.

DODGE CHALLENGER

F ord pulled off a masterstroke with the unveiling of its 2005 Mustang, heavily inspired by the 1960s original, so Dodge reckoned it could perform the same trick with its Challenger concept. Harking back to the glory days of the 1960s when muscle cars ruled, Dodge attempted to give its image a boost with this updated pony car. Using the production Chrysler 300C as its basis, the 21st-century Challenger retained the same proportions and overall lines as its ancestor – and even the colour scheme was carried over for maximum nostalgia. It's easy to say such exploitation is cynical – but you have to admit the car looked fabulous!

SPECIFICATIONS

ENGINE CAPACITY:	6100 cc
CONFIGURATION:	front-mounted petrol V8
POWER:	317 kW (425 bhp)
TOP SPEED:	280 km/h (174 mph)
TRANSMISSION:	six-speed manual, rear-wheel drive
LENGTH:	5025 mm (197.83 in)
WIDTH:	1997 mm (78.62 in)
DEBUT:	Detroit 2006

There was only one engine that could be fitted to the Challenger – the legendary Hemi V8 in 6.1-litre form, with 317 kW (425 bhp).

The Challenger wasn't an especially big car, but there was space for four adults inside, each with their own bucket seat.

Although the V8 was very simply engineered, it could produce up to 569 N m (420 lb ft) of torque, giving a zero to 60 mph (97 km/h) time of 4.5 seconds.

Those stripes on the bonnet (hood) recall the Challenger's heyday; they were exposed carbon fibre rather than black paint.

Giving the car its ultra-smooth lines there was flush-fitting glass all round, with no B-pillar and integral bumpers front and rear.

FIAT TREPIUNO

During Fiat's first century of building cars, it enjoyed a huge slice of the home market and profits were easily attained. This had all changed, however, by the time the Trepiuno surfaced at the 2004 Geneva motor show; the company was in trouble and needed to pull something out of the hat – and fast. Returning to its small-car roots, Fiat found the chance to do what it's best at with the Trepiuno – producing urban cars that look great and are a buzz to drive. With lines clearly based on those of the iconic Fiat 500, the Trepiuno could be just what Fiat needs to save itself from oblivion.

SPECIFICATIONS

ENGINE CAPACITY:	n/a
CONFIGURATION:	front-mounted
POWER:	n/a
TOP SPEED:	n/a
TRANSMISSION:	front-wheel drive
LENGTH:	3300 mm (129.92 in)
WIDTH:	n/a
DEBUT:	Geneva 2004
DESIGNER:	Roberto Giolito

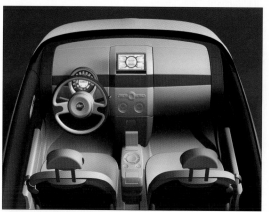

The dashboard could be folded forward on the offside, allowing the seat to move forward, creating extra space behind.

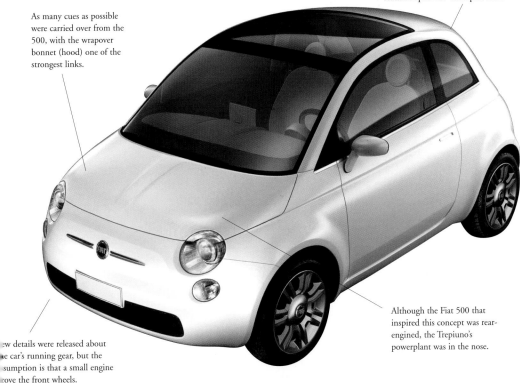

The name Trepiuno came from the car's unusual seating configuration, which featured space for 'three plus one'.

As many cues as possible were carried over from the 500, with the wrapover bonnet (hood) one of the strongest links.

Although the Fiat 500 that inspired this concept was rear-engined, the Trepiuno's powerplant was in the nose.

ew details were released about e car's running gear, but the sumption is that a small engine rove the front wheels.

FORD KA

Perhaps even more radical in showroom form than as a concept, the Ford Ka was a breath of fresh air at a time when car design was getting boring and predictable. Ford's chief European small-car designer Fritz Mayhew spotted a bottle of Evian water in a restaurant. Jagged mountains etched along the top of the bottle reminded Mayhew of an edgy design that Ford's German studio had just proposed for a new European small car. Mayhew took the Evian bottle back to Ford's Dunton (England) design studio that afternoon in early 1994, and it became one of the influences of the sharp design theme of the Ford Ka.

SPECIFICATIONS

ENGINE CAPACITY:	non-runner
CONFIGURATION:	front-mounted
POWER:	n/a
TOP SPEED:	n/a
TRANSMISSION:	n/a
LENGTH:	3350 mm (131.89 in)
WIDTH:	1640 mm (64.57 in)
DEBUT:	Geneva 1994
DESIGNER:	Claude Lobo

The baby of the Ford range, the Ka carried all the New-Edge design cues with which its bigger siblings would be blessed.

It was hoped a two-stroke Orbital engine, or a small diesel, would provide the power. Electric power was considered, but rejected.

The shape of the Ka didn't change significantly in the transition to production car, although the nose was made more aerodynamic.

The original concept wasn't fitted with an interior. That was the easy bit after gaining acceptance for the exterior.

Ka concept was unveiled non-runner; it was saged that nothing more a four-cylinder engine uld be fitted.

129

JAGUAR F-TYPE

How a company with Jaguar's heritage could produce a concept as beautiful as the F-Type, then not put it into production, is beyond comprehension. The F-type was a development of the XK180 shown in 1999. But whereas Jaguars had become rather portly thanks to somewhat generous dimensions, this concept intended to reverse the trend. The F-type had started out as a project overseen by Jaguar's then head of design Geoff Lawson. But when Lawson died suddenly in June 1999, Keith Helfet became the design project leader, and the result of his team's efforts was one of the most beautiful concepts ever seen.

SPECIFICATIONS

ENGINE CAPACITY:	2967 cc
CONFIGURATION:	front-engined V6 petrol
POWER:	179 kW (240 bhp)
TOP SPEED:	n/a
TRANSMISSION:	five-speed auto, rear-wheel drive
LENGTH:	4115 mm (162.01 in)
WIDTH:	1732 mm (68.19 in)
DEBUT:	Detroit 2000
DESIGN HEAD:	Keith Helfet

Using classic Jaguar styling cues, the F-Type was as curvaceous and inviting as the E-Type that was launched nearly 40 years before it.

It looked as though a massive, hugely powerful engine was fitted, but there was just a 3-litre V6, rated at 179 kW (240 bhp).

The interior was simple, but it didn't look cheap. There was plenty of aluminium trim, machined from solid billets, then polished to perfection.

The show car featured no weather protection at all – engineering a full roof would have spoiled the car's lines.

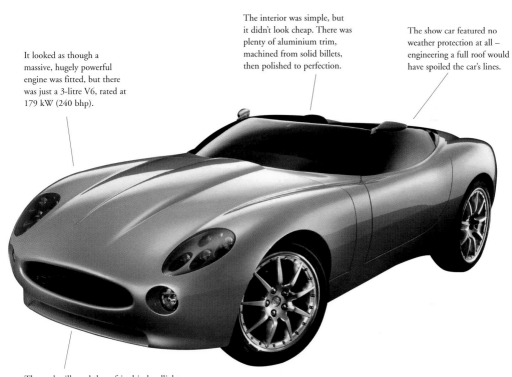

The oval grille and those faired-in headlights were inspired by early E-Types. The same went for the haunches over the rear wheels.

LAMBORGHINI CALA

Code-named P140 and designed by Italdesign, the Cala was going to be Lamborghini's replacement for its small car, the Jalpa. However, while the Jalpa was powered by a 3.5-litre V8, the Cala packed a 4-litre V10 punch amidships. It would be several years before Lamborghini committed itself to a small car along these lines, with the Gallardo appearing in 2003 and being the first car from Sant Agata to be fitted with a V10 engine. The Gallardo was also the model that went on to become Lamborghini's biggest-selling model ever; if only the company had been more courageous in the mid-1990s…

SPECIFICATIONS

ENGINE CAPACITY:	3900 cc
CONFIGURATION:	mid-mounted V10
POWER:	298 kw (400 bhp)
TOP SPEED:	291 km/h (181 mph)
TRANSMISSION:	six-speed manual, rear-wheel drive
LENGTH:	4390 mm (172.83 in)
WIDTH:	1900 mm (74.80 in)
DEBUT:	Geneva 1995

The Cala's construction was ultra-modern, with its bonded aluminium monocoque which was both light and strong.

The roof panel was removable, while its leading edge also featured glass inserts to lighten up the interior.

Mounted in the middle there was a 3900-cc V10 engine, which could develop up to 298 kW (400 bhp).

As befitted a luxury sports car, the interior was beautifully trimmed in leather. Two colours featured: claret and tan.

The power was sent to the rear wheels only, via a six-speed manual gearbox; there was no sequential shift.

LAMBORGHINI MIURA

When your portfolio contains perhaps the most beautiful car ever to turn a wheel, it's only natural that you're going to turn to it for inspiration at some point. When Lamborghini did just that with its Miura concept at the 2006 Detroit motor show, however, it didn't count on the negative feedback. Built to celebrate the fortieth anniversary of the production Miura's debut, the Miura concept was merely an update of the earlier design. Lamborghini said it was prepared to put the car into production if enough people asked it to, but instead of praise being showered on the company for its Miura concept, Lamborghini was accused of cynically cashing in on its heritage.

SPECIFICATIONS

ENGINE CAPACITY:	non-runner
CONFIGURATION:	mid-engined
POWER:	n/a
TOP SPEED:	n/a
TRANSMISSION:	n/a
LENGTH:	n/a
WIDTH:	n/a
DEBUT:	Detroit 2006
DESIGNER:	Walter de Silva

Subtly updated, this concept's roots are instantly recognizable, with those aggressive rear haunches and lithe front end. The slats over the rear window were a copy of those on the original car; they allowed hot air to escape from the engine bay.

The original Miura featured pop-up headlights, but these had been banned by 2006. Consequently, faired-in units were fitted.

No mechanicals were fitted as this was just a mock-up; however, a V12 would have been fitted in the event of production.

The scoops in the sills were to feed cooling air to the mid-mounted powerplant; so were the vents positioned just behind the doors.

135

LANCIA DIALOGOS

The aim of the Dialogos was to bring something new to the luxury car market, with soft, flowing lines, an innovative, spacious interior and Italian engineering that would ensure the car was also a joy to drive. A fundamental part of the idea behind the car was that the occupants would meld with the car, in effect having a dialogue with it – which is why the concept was so named. The Dialogos offered the perfect fusion of past and future, with many of the design details being inspired by cars from Lancia's rich heritage – and it later went into production (albeit in watered-down form) as the Thesis.

SPECIFICATIONS

ENGINE CAPACITY:	n/a
CONFIGURATION:	front-mounted
POWER:	n/a
TOP SPEED:	n/a
TRANSMISSION:	front-wheel drive
LENGTH:	4990 mm (196.46 in)
WIDTH:	1950 mm (76.77 in)
DEBUT:	Turin 1998
DESIGN HEAD:	Mike Robinson

The interior resembled something you'd find in an expensively furnished apartment, with soft leather and Alcantara throughout.

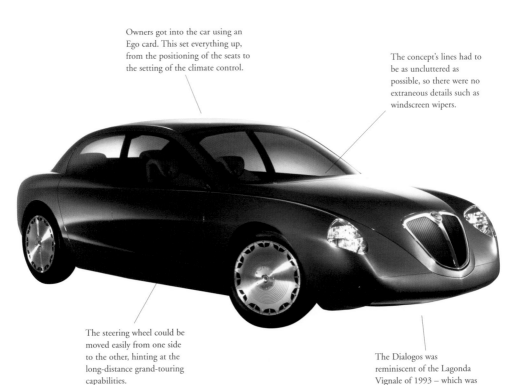

Owners got into the car using an Ego card. This set everything up, from the positioning of the seats to the setting of the climate control.

The concept's lines had to be as uncluttered as possible, so there were no extraneous details such as windscreen wipers.

The steering wheel could be moved easily from one side to the other, hinting at the long-distance grand-touring capabilities.

The Dialogos was reminiscent of the Lagonda Vignale of 1993 – which was no bad thing as it was graceful and unfussy.

137

LANCIA FULVIETTA

It may have been heavily reliant on the iconic Fulvia for its lines, but the Lancia Fulvietta was no worse off for it. Superbly updating the beautifully styled coupé of the 1960s and 1970s, the Fulvietta would reach the showrooms in much the same guise as it was shown at the Frankfurt motor show in 2003, according to talk. As usual for Lancia, the company's managers couldn't make up their minds whether or not to build it, while potential customers queued impatiently, chequebooks in hand. How there could be any indecision is beyond comprehension; this was one of the most beautiful cars ever to come from Lancia.

SPECIFICATIONS

ENGINE CAPACITY:	1.8 litres
CONFIGURATION:	front-mounted in-line petrol four-cylinder
POWER:	138 kW (185 bhp)
TOP SPEED:	209 km/h (130 mph)
TRANSMISSION:	six-speed manual, front-wheel drive
LENGTH:	4295 mm (169.09 in)
WIDTH:	1725 mm (67.91 in)
DEBUT:	Frankfurt 2003

Although the proportions hardly varied between the old car (Fulvia) and the new (Fulvietta), the track was wider for greater stability.

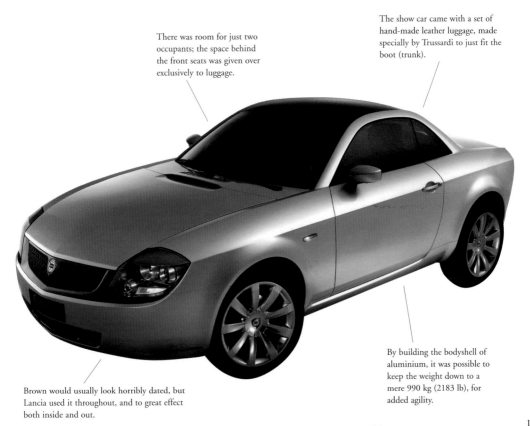

There was room for just two occupants; the space behind the front seats was given over exclusively to luggage.

The show car came with a set of hand-made leather luggage, made specially by Trussardi to just fit the boot (trunk).

Brown would usually look horribly dated, but Lancia used it throughout, and to great effect both inside and out.

By building the bodyshell of aluminium, it was possible to keep the weight down to a mere 990 kg (2183 lb), for added agility.

139

LAND ROVER RANGE STORMER

If you're looking for a classic case of how concept cars are watered down before reaching the showroom, here's the perfect example. While the Range Rover Sport was the production version of the Stormer, the concept car's amazing lines were almost completely lost in the transition. This was Land Rover's first ever concept car, more than half a century after the company started car production – many of the styling cues incorporated into the Range Stormer harked back to the first Range Rover of 1970. Still, while many of the styling elements looked back, the technology incorporated in the Stormer was very much about the future.

SPECIFICATIONS

ENGINE CAPACITY:	n/a
CONFIGURATION:	front-mounted V8 petrol
POWER:	n/a
TOP SPEED:	n/a
TRANSMISSION:	four-wheel drive, six-speed semiauto
LENGTH:	n/a
WIDTH:	n/a
DEBUT:	Detroit 2004
DESIGN HEAD:	Geoff Upex

The original Range Rover had been a workhorse; this new car, however, was much more about on-road driving pleasure.

The 'floating roof' was another Range Rover trademark, initially seen on the first cars that went on sale in 1970.

The glasshouse was narrow, and emphasized by the high waistline to give the Stormer a very tough look.

The bluff nose featured a deep front air dam and those jewel-effect stepped headlights that were a Land Rover trademark.

The Range Stormer was intended to deliver on-road sportiness, which is why it featured 559-mm (22-in) low-profile tyres.

LEXUS LF-A

W e'd already seen the LF-S, LF-C and LF-X concepts at earlier events; at the 2005 Detroit motor show it was the turn of the LF-A supercar to burst onto the scene. Unlike the situation with its siblings, however, development of the LF-A was to be continued by Lexus, with a view to putting it on sale to take on such greats as the Porsche 911 and Aston Martin V8 Vantage. This was the fourth car to use what Lexus termed its 'L-Finesse' styling theme, which balanced simple, uncluttered lines with a hint of aggression. It didn't matter how Lexus dressed it up, though, many people still thought it looked like an overblown Toyota Celica …

SPECIFICATIONS

ENGINE CAPACITY:	5.0 litres
CONFIGURATION:	front-mounted petrol V8 or V10
POWER:	373 kW (500 bhp) plus
TOP SPEED:	322 km/h (200 mph) plus
TRANSMISSION:	semi-auto, rear-wheel drive
LENGTH:	4400 mm (173.23 in)
WIDTH:	1860 mm (73.23 in)
DEBUT:	Detroit 2005

The satellite navigation included maps of the world's major race circuits, so drivers could plot their position as they drove round.

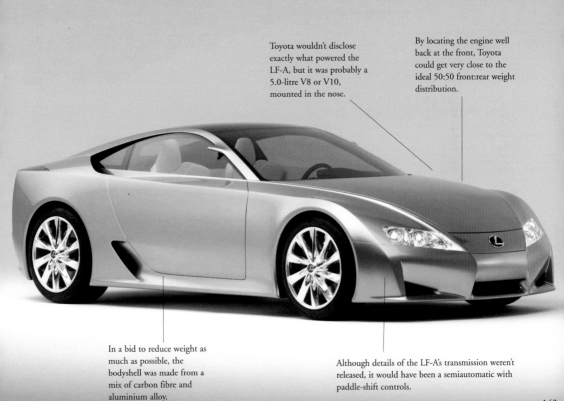

Toyota wouldn't disclose exactly what powered the LF-A, but it was probably a 5.0-litre V8 or V10, mounted in the nose.

By locating the engine well back at the front, Toyota could get very close to the ideal 50:50 front:rear weight distribution.

In a bid to reduce weight as much as possible, the bodyshell was made from a mix of carbon fibre and aluminium alloy.

Although details of the LF-A's transmission weren't released, it would have been a semiautomatic with paddle-shift controls.

143

MAZDA RX-EVOLV

The RX-Evolv, which was tasked with injecting new life into the rotary engine for Mazda, was first shown at the 1999 Tokyo motor show. At that stage there were rumours that this could be a new combination of sports and family car which would see production in the new millennium, but nobody was sure. It was pretty radical, with its 'FreeStyle' rear-hinged back doors and tiny slitted front lights – but these were the type of details which would soon be dispensed with if the project went any further. Except, of course, in the case of the door arrangement; the RX-8 did use the same system when it became a production reality.

The idea was copied elsewhere, but those rear-hinged rear doors work better on the RX-Evolv than on most other concepts.

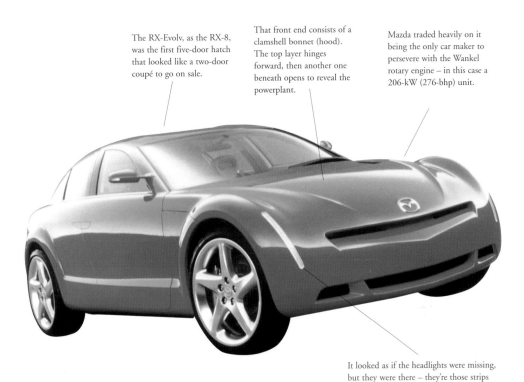

The RX-Evolv, as the RX-8, was the first five-door hatch that looked like a two-door coupé to go on sale.

That front end consists of a clamshell bonnet (hood). The top layer hinges forward, then another one beneath opens to reveal the powerplant.

Mazda traded heavily on it being the only car maker to persevere with the Wankel rotary engine – in this case a 206-kW (276-bhp) unit.

It looked as if the headlights were missing, but they were there – they're those strips along the front edge of the wings (fenders).

MAZDA KABURA

W ith the RX-8 selling like hot cakes and the third generation of MX-5 just having been launched, you might think that Mazda had enough sports cars in its range – especially with the MX-5 already having become the world's best-selling roadster. When the Kabura was unveiled at the 2006 Detroit motor show, however, Mazda spoke very seriously about the car potentially reaching the showroom – albeit with some significant changes. The main reason for this was the fact that the Kabura was asymmetrical; as well as a cabin with a '3 + 1' seating arrangement, there was just one door on the driver's side, but two on the passengers'.

SPECIFICATIONS

ENGINE CAPACITY:	1999 cc
CONFIGURATION:	front-mounted in-line petrol four-cylinder
POWER:	118 kW (158 bhp)
TOP SPEED:	n/a
TRANSMISSION:	six-speed manual, rear-wheel drive
LENGTH:	4050 mm (159.45 in)
WIDTH:	1780 mm (70.08 in)
DEBUT:	Detroit 2006

The Kabura looked larger than it was; it wasn't much bigger than the diminutive MX-5, as it was short and narrow.

The tailgate opened in two sections. The top section was conventionally hinged, while the bottom one opened to the side.

The cabin featured a front passenger seat that sat 15 cm (six inches) ahead of the driver, to increase rear seat legroom on one side.

Mazda didn't need to come up with a fresh engine; the four-cylinder unit mounted in the nose was taken straight from the MX-5.

This was intended to be a budget sports car, but those wheels weren't cheap. They were 483 mm (19 in) across at the front and 508 mm (20 in) at the rear.

MCC SMART

The problem with concept cars is that they show what's possible if risks are taken – but they always get watered down and, by the time they reach the showroom, they're a shadow of their former selves. But there are exceptions, and the MCC Smart is one of them. The project started as a collaboration between Swatch and Volkswagen, but the latter bailed out, leaving Swatch to team up with Daimler-Benz. By the time the car went on sale, Swatch had also bailed out, leaving Daimler-Benz to go it alone. Amazingly, this traditionally conservative company had the courage to put the Smart into production, and even grow the range – unsuccessfully.

SPECIFICATIONS

ENGINE CAPACITY:	n/a
CONFIGURATION:	rear-mounted three-cylinder petrol
POWER:	n/a
TOP SPEED:	140 km/h (87 mph)
TRANSMISSION:	sequential manual, rear-wheel drive
LENGTH:	2500 mm (98.43 in)
WIDTH:	1500 mm (59.06 in)
DEBUT:	March 1993

The Eco-Speedster was the open-topped version of MCC's Smart car – there was also a closed version called the Eco-Sprinter.

The driver sat slightly ahead of the passenger, so that they weren't both trying to use the same shoulder space.

This was to be the ultimate city car, which is why it was just 2500 mm (98.43 in) long and 1500 mm (59.06 in) wide.

Sitting at the back of the Eco-Speedster was a three-cylinder petrol engine, which drove through a sequential manual gearbox.

Despite the car's size, safety was paramount – although the three-layer chassis would cause big problems in production.

MERCEDES-BENZ A93

When the Vision A93 was first seen, everybody knew how significant it was – this car would take Mercedes into markets it had never even thought about before, with the launch of the A-Class. Mercedes was used to selling premium large cars, not small hatchbacks; it was the car that would steal sales from the likes of Volkswagen. The Vision was also important because it was touted as the most innovative small car since the original Issigonis-designed Mini of 1959, thanks to some cutting-edge packaging. Three versions were built initially – diesel, petrol and electric – but only the first two would enter production.

SPECIFICATIONS

ENGINE CAPACITY:	550 volts A/C
CONFIGURATION:	electric
POWER:	40 kW (54 bhp)
TOP SPEED:	121 km/h (75 mph)
TRANSMISSION:	automatic
LENGTH:	3327 mm (130.98 in)
WIDTH:	n/a
DEBUT:	Frankfurt 1993

The high seating position helped to improve visibility, but it also raised the centre of gravity, which would lead to instability problems.

Three versions of the A93 were built: a diesel, a petrol and an electric one. Ultimately, only the former two were offered.

There was flexible seating – the A93 combined city car and MPV characteristics so that it could carry any combination of luggage or people.

It looked more radical than the car which made it to production, but the stance was just the same: a narrow track and high roof.

Beneath the cabin was a dual-level chassis, housing the engine and gearbox. In a collision, they would stay out of the car's interior.

MERCEDES-BENZ SLK

A lthough the SLK is often credited with the introduction of the folding hard top, the concept that was first seen at the 1993 Turin motor show wasn't fitted with a roof of any kind. And although the SLK was several decades behind cars from Peugeot and Ford that used the same roof construction, here was a folding metal roof that was reliable, leak-free and easy to use. The concept was called the SLK Studie, with the S short for 'Sporty', the L for 'Lightweight' and the K for 'Kurz', the German word for 'short'. It showed what a smaller, more affordable Mercedes SL would look like.

SPECIFICATIONS

ENGINE CAPACITY:	2100 cc
CONFIGURATION:	front-mounted in-line four petrol
POWER:	119 kW (150 bhp)
TOP SPEED:	209 km/h (130 mph)
TRANSMISSION:	five-speed manual, rear-wheel drive
LENGTH:	4090 mm (161.02 in)
WIDTH:	1720 mm (67.72 in)
DEBUT:	Turin 1994
DESIGNER:	Peter Arcadipane

There were two SLK concepts: the first was painted silver, while the second one (with the folding metal roof) was blue.

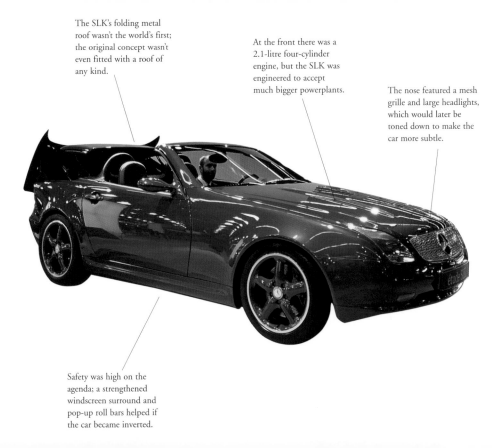

The SLK's folding metal roof wasn't the world's first; the original concept wasn't even fitted with a roof of any kind.

At the front there was a 2.1-litre four-cylinder engine, but the SLK was engineered to accept much bigger powerplants.

The nose featured a mesh grille and large headlights, which would later be toned down to make the car more subtle.

Safety was high on the agenda; a strengthened windscreen surround and pop-up roll bars helped if the car became inverted.

MINI TRAVELLER

To celebrate the forty-fifth anniversary of the original Traveller's launch, Mini unveiled its 21st-century interpretation at the 2005 Frankfurt motor show. The second of three Traveller concepts (the others were unveiled at Tokyo in 2005 and Detroit in 2006), this version carried the same theme as the others: space with style. Interestingly, although everyone knew the cars as the Traveller concepts, BMW never made any such references – instead they were named after the event at which they were shown. And the reason for this? BMW didn't know who owned the Traveller name, so it couldn't risk a lawsuit for copyright infringement.

SPECIFICATIONS

ENGINE CAPACITY:	n/a
CONFIGURATION:	front-mounted in-line petrol four-cylinder
POWER:	n/a
TOP SPEED:	n/a
TRANSMISSION:	front-wheel drive
LENGTH:	n/a
WIDTH:	n/a
DEBUT:	Frankfurt 2005

The rear doors were fixed to the bodywork via parallelogram joints, ensuring the best possible access to the load bay.

Mini has already confirmed that the Traveller will go into production, but some of the more costly details will be watered down.

To increase seat legroom as much as possible, the front seats were 'floating', and fixed to the car's structure via the central console.

Expensive materials finished in light colours were used throughout the interior, in a bid to make it feel more spacious than it really was.

The double-hinged doors moved away from the car's bodywork as they were opened, allowing for easier access to the rear seats.

PONTIAC AZTEK

Crossover vehicles were becoming increasingly popular by the end of the twentieth century, which was no surprise as these were the cars which combined two or more sectors to give the best of all. Or the worst if things didn't quite go to plan. With the Aztek, Pontiac tried to combine the best attributes of a mid-sized saloon, a van and a sport utility vehicle – with the latter becoming increasingly popular in the United States at the time. So what a shame that Phil Kucera designed such a hideous car which few took seriously. Even more tragically, the Aztek then went into production with the exterior design barely changed.

SPECIFICATIONS

ENGINE CAPACITY: 3.4-litre
CONFIGURATION: front-mounted V6 petrol
POWER: 149 kW (200 bhp)
TOP SPEED: 180 km/h (112 mph)
TRANSMISSION: four-speed auto, front-wheel drive
LENGTH: 4546 mm (178.98 in)
WIDTH: 1956 mm (77.01 in)
DEBUT: Detroit 1999
DESIGNER: Phil Kucera

The Aztec looks disfigured from this angle, but there isn't a view of the vehicle that makes it appear any more flattering.

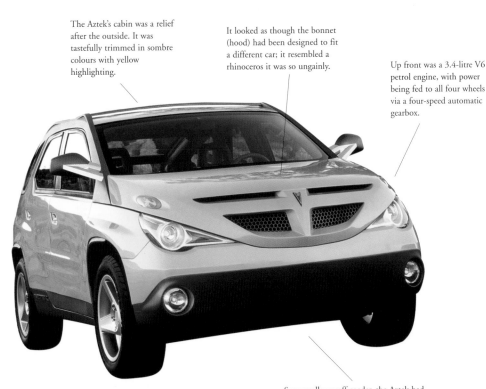

The Aztek's cabin was a relief after the outside. It was tastefully trimmed in sombre colours with yellow highlighting.

It looked as though the bonnet (hood) had been designed to fit a different car; it resembled a rhinoceros it was so ungainly.

Up front was a 3.4-litre V6 petrol engine, with power being fed to all four wheels via a four-speed automatic gearbox.

Supposedly an off-roader, the Aztek had monocoque construction and minimal ground clearance that meant it was better on the road.

PORSCHE BOXSTER

As soon as the Porsche Boxster was shown at the 1993 Detroit motor show, it was clear that this was much more than just a design study. Porsche was going to put the car into production as long as enough interest was shown – and, sure enough, very quickly the deposits came in thick and fast. But many of those who put their cheque in before the final production car was shown were disappointed. Between the concept and production stages the Boxster's design was toned down, and there were many people who decided that the road car was too tame after such a beautifully detailed show car had been displayed.

SPECIFICATIONS

ENGINE CAPACITY:	2855 cc
CONFIGURATION:	mid-mounted flat-six petrol
POWER:	186 kW (49 bhp)
TOP SPEED:	257 km/h (160 mph)
TRANSMISSION:	manual, rear-wheel drive
LENGTH:	4115 mm (162.01 in)
WIDTH:	1778 mm (70 in)
DEBUT:	Detroit 1993
DESIGNER:	Grant Larson

The shape of the Boxster was reminiscent of two Porsche classics: the 550 Spyder and the RSK. But that was certainly no bad thing.

The 2855-cc flat-six gave 186 kW (249 bhp), which was enough for a top speed of 257 km/h (160 mph) and a zero to 100 km/h (62 mph) time of around six seconds.

The interior was simple but beautifully detailed. The LCD in the dash was modern, which contrasted with the alloy air vents.

Details such as the front spoiler and sill air intakes were lost in the transition from concept to production car.

Although the Boxster was compact, its wheelbase was longer than a 911's. That gave excellent handling with a decent ride.

RENAULT SCENIC

The Renault Scenic has become an integral part of the new car market, having launched a whole raft of imitations. But when the concept was first shown at the 1991 Frankfurt show, it was completely fresh. It would be another three years before Citroën had its own version on show (the Xanae), and, while the production Scenic wasn't as radical as the concept, the overall themes were far-reaching. The whole point of the Scenic was to offer unprecedented levels of space, but without the car being any bigger on the road than a conventional small family hatch. The fact the Scenic is much emulated shows just what a brilliant idea it was.

SPECIFICATIONS

ENGINE CAPACITY:	1998 cc
CONFIGURATION:	front-mounted petrol in-line four-cylinder
POWER:	112 kW (150 bhp)
TOP SPEED:	183 km/h (114 mph)
TRANSMISSION:	four-speed automatic, four-wheel drive
LENGTH:	4150 mm (163.39 in)
WIDTH:	1920 mm (75.59 in)
DEBUT:	Frankfurt 1991

To enable easier entry and exit in confined spaces for both driver and passengers, both the front and the rear doors of the Scenic slid open.

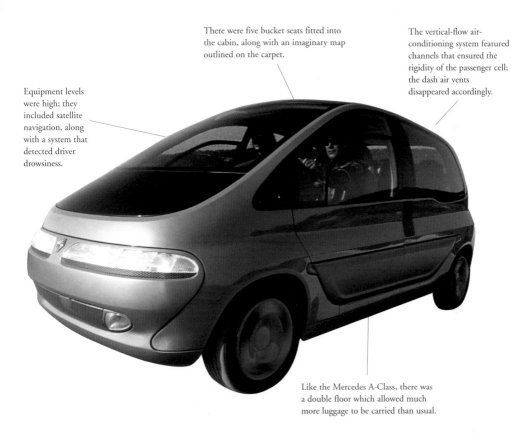

There were five bucket seats fitted into the cabin, along with an imaginary map outlined on the carpet.

The vertical-flow air-conditioning system featured channels that ensured the rigidity of the passenger cell; the dash air vents disappeared accordingly.

Equipment levels were high; they included satellite navigation, along with a system that detected driver drowsiness.

Like the Mercedes A-Class, there was a double floor which allowed much more luggage to be carried than usual.

RENAULT VEL SATIS

Termed a four-seat coupé de ville by Renault, the Vel Satis was avant-garde in both concept and design. Whereas most luxury cars of the time were conventional three-box saloons, Renault's aim was to move towards a monobox design. So where most executive cars were equipped with a boot (trunk), Renault's take on the genre was that there should be a silhouette more akin to a people-carrier or estate car (station wagon). The name is taken from the words 'velocity' and 'satisfaction', which may seem like an odd pairing, but hints at the speed and comfort which are the car's foremost attributes.

SPECIFICATIONS

ENGINE CAPACITY:	2946 cc
CONFIGURATION:	front-mounted V6 petrol
POWER:	158 kW (210 bhp)
TOP SPEED:	225 km/h (140 mph)
TRANSMISSION:	five-speed sequential manual
LENGTH:	4680 mm (184.25 in)
WIDTH:	1880 mm (74.02 in)
DEBUT:	Paris 1998

The Vel Satis's interior featured wood and leather, but despite such traditional materials the design was very modern.

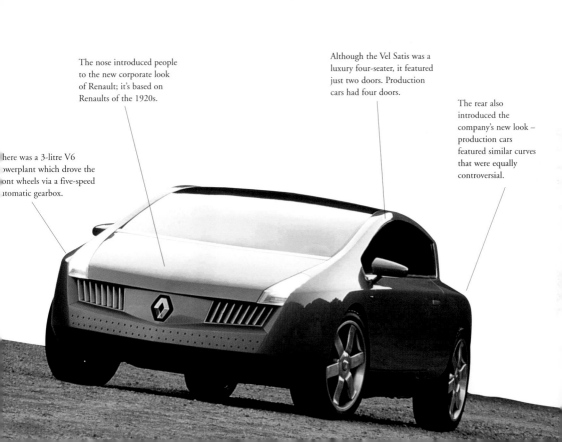

The nose introduced people to the new corporate look of Renault; it's based on Renaults of the 1920s.

Although the Vel Satis was a luxury four-seater, it featured just two doors. Production cars had four doors.

The rear also introduced the company's new look – production cars featured similar curves that were equally controversial.

here was a 3-litre V6 owerplant which drove the ont wheels via a five-speed utomatic gearbox.

ROLLS-ROYCE 100EX/101EX

Rolls-Royce didn't do concepts – or at least not until it became part of the BMW group. While prototypes and experimental cars had come from the company before (all carrying EX tags), this was the first time the company had given audiences an early view of its future two-door cars. In early 2004 we all caught a glimpse of the fully working 100EX two-door convertible prototype; two years later we got to see the 101EX coupé equivalent. Although Rolls-Royce maintained with both cars that neither would reach production, the reality is that cars very similar to them would go on sale not many years after.

SPECIFICATIONS

ENGINE CAPACITY:	9001 cc
CONFIGURATION:	front-mounted petrol V16
POWER:	n/a
TOP SPEED:	n/a
TRANSMISSION:	six-speed auto, rear-wheel drive
LENGTH:	5669 mm (223.19 in)
WIDTH:	1990 mm (78.35 in)
DEBUT:	Geneva 2004
DESIGNER:	Marek Djordjevic

There were just two doors fitted, and they were rear-hinged. Rolls-Royce coined the term 'coach doors' for them.

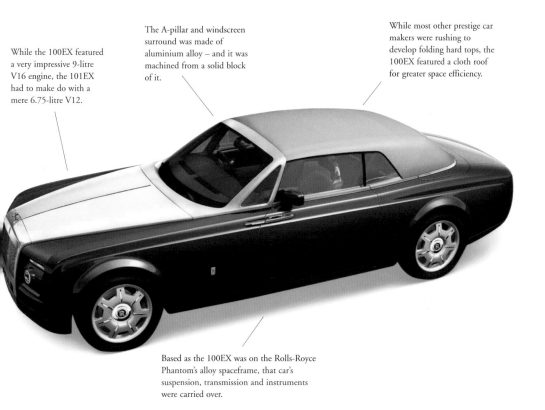

While the 100EX featured a very impressive 9-litre V16 engine, the 101EX had to make do with a mere 6.75-litre V12.

The A-pillar and windscreen surround was made of aluminium alloy – and it was machined from a solid block of it.

While most other prestige car makers were rushing to develop folding hard tops, the 100EX featured a cloth roof for greater space efficiency.

Based as the 100EX was on the Rolls-Royce Phantom's alloy spaceframe, that car's suspension, transmission and instruments were carried over.

ROVER TCV

The TCV was Rover's demonstration that it was on the way back up after a prolonged period of uncertainty. Ever since Rover had been sold by BMW for a token £10, few had much faith in the company's chances of survival – the TCV had much to prove. Rover claimed the rather unimaginatively named Tourer Concept Vehicle combined luxury, style and driving enjoyment with exceptional practicality and adaptability. It certainly managed that because its interior was built to be so flexible that you could carry just about anything, whatever its shape. When the car made its debut it even had a washing machine stuffed into the load bay, sitting upright.

SPECIFICATIONS

ENGINE CAPACITY:	2497 cc
CONFIGURATION:	front-mounted V6 petrol
POWER:	130 kW (174 bhp)
TOP SPEED:	n/a
TRANSMISSION:	five-speed semiauto, front-wheel drive
LENGTH:	4500 mm (177.17 in)
WIDTH:	n/a
DEBUT:	Geneva 2002
DESIGNER:	Peter Stevens

The tapering roofline aided the aerodynamics and aesthetics. The boot (trunk) floor could be lowered to increase luggage bay space.

Aiming to offer practicality, adaptability, luxury and style, the TCV signalled a new design direction for MG-Rover. It certainly looked modern.

There were lots of seating configurations for carrying passengers and hauling luggage – loads up to three metres (10 ft) long could be carried.

ROVER

The front end was the least flattering of all the car's angles. The large headlights vie with the oversized grille for prominence.

The Rover 75-based TCV was a non-runner, but a 2.5-litre V6 engine would be fitted, with four-wheel drive.

SEAT SALSA

U ntil Volkswagen took a controlling stake in SEAT in 1985, the Spanish company did little more than build its own versions of Fiat's cast-offs. But with SEAT unveiling one concept after another from the early 1990s, it was clear that there was plenty of life in the company – and the Salsa demonstrated this better than anything. The VW Group was trying to make SEAT synonymous with sportiness, and the Salsa reinforced that, while just oozing character. At the 2000 Paris motor show the Salsa was developed further to become the Salsa Emoción – a jacked-up four-wheel drive derivative designed to take on the Renault Scenic RX4.

SPECIFICATIONS

ENGINE CAPACITY:	2791 cc
CONFIGURATION:	front-mounted V6 petrol
POWER:	186 kW (250 bhp)
TOP SPEED:	245 km/h (152 mph)
TRANSMISSION:	five-speed semiauto, four-wheel drive
LENGTH:	4152 mm (163.46 in)
WIDTH:	1777 mm (69.96 in)
DEBUT:	Geneva 2000

The Salsa made an everyday, affordable mid-sized hatch into something that looked enticing and completely modern – if not futuristic.

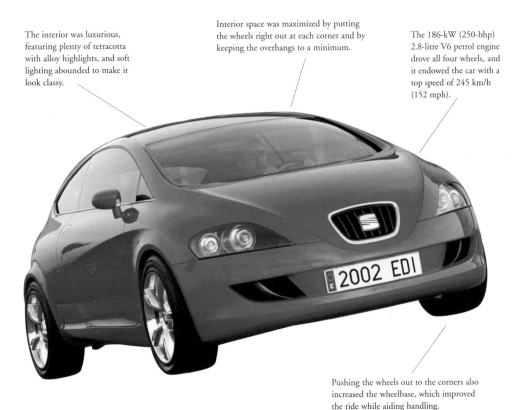

The interior was luxurious, featuring plenty of terracotta with alloy highlights, and soft lighting abounded to make it look classy.

Interior space was maximized by putting the wheels right out at each corner and by keeping the overhangs to a minimum.

The 186-kW (250-bhp) 2.8-litre V6 petrol engine drove all four wheels, and it endowed the car with a top speed of 245 km/h (152 mph).

2002 EDI

Pushing the wheels out to the corners also increased the wheelbase, which improved the ride while aiding handling.

VAUXHALL ANTARA GTC

For years, General Motors' design departments were in the doldrums. While everybody else was busy churning out cars with character, GM's various divisions were trying to see how little imagination they could get away with when their production cars were unveiled. The Antara GTC aimed to change all that, with sharp lines and imaginative features – and it worked brilliantly. Here was a car that was guaranteed to go into production, yet which looked fabulous from every angle. So what a shame that, when the production car was unveiled just a few months later, it was just a former shadow of its concept cousin.

SPECIFICATIONS

ENGINE CAPACITY:	1.9-litre twin-turbo
CONFIGURATION:	front-mounted in-line four-cylinder turbodiesel
POWER:	158 kW (212 bhp)
TOP SPEED:	211 km/h (131 mph)
TRANSMISSION:	six-speed semiauto, four-wheel drive
LENGTH:	4530 mm (178.35 in)
WIDTH:	1970 mm (77.56 in)
DEBUT:	Frankfurt 2005

The Antara GTC's tailgate featured a pantographic hinge, which meant it moved away from the body when it was opened.

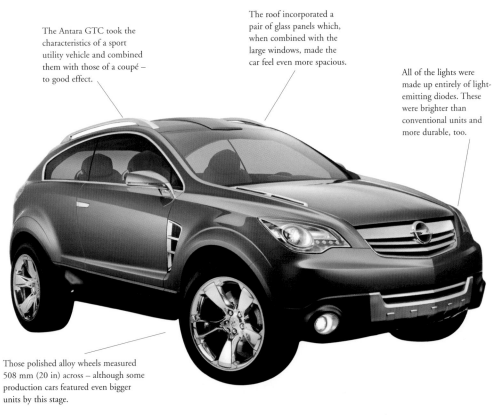

The Antara GTC took the characteristics of a sport utility vehicle and combined them with those of a coupé – to good effect.

The roof incorporated a pair of glass panels which, when combined with the large windows, made the car feel even more spacious.

All of the lights were made up entirely of light-emitting diodes. These were brighter than conventional units and more durable, too.

Those polished alloy wheels measured 508 mm (20 in) across – although some production cars featured even bigger units by this stage.

171

VOLKSWAGEN CONCEPT 1 (BEETLE)

When the Concept 1 was first shown, the original Beetle was still in production, in Mexico. But although the rear-engined air-cooled classic was still rolling off the production lines, it wasn't officially available in many markets around the world. What was needed was an updated version with the cheeky looks of the classic Beetle, but with modern standards of driveability, crash safety and environmental friendliness. Such factors were the driving force behind the first Concept 1 – VW's sales were falling in the United States, and a new car with a funky design was just what the company needed to put itself back on the map. People had forgotten the company was still selling cars!

SPECIFICATIONS

ENGINE CAPACITY:	1896 cc turbocharged
CONFIGURATION:	front-mounted in-line four diesel
POWER:	82 kW (110 bhp)
TOP SPEED:	179 km/h (111 mph)
TRANSMISSION:	five-speed Ecomatic
LENGTH:	3824 mm (150.55 in)
WIDTH:	1633 mm (64.29 in)
DEBUT:	Detroit 1994
DESIGNER:	J Mays

At the turn of the twentieth century, retro design was rife – so VW cashed in on the fact it made the best-selling car ever.

There would be a water-cooled engine, mounted at the front and driving the front wheels. The first concept was a non-runner, though.

The design roots were obvious, and, although the mechanical configuration of the new car was completely different, it worked.

The equipment count was high, with air bags, air conditioning and a stereo system, but the design was very retro.

The Concept 1 looked cute with its narrow 457-mm (18-in) diameter wheels. By the time the car reached production, smaller wheels were fitted.

CONCEPT
VOLKSWAGEN

VOLVO ECC

Looking like the S80 of 1998, the Environmental Concept Car was first seen as far back as 1992. The brief was to design a car which offered quality, safety, comfort and performance, but which would also be environmentally friendly. The car's design would allow a drag coefficient of just 0.25, although the final result was a Cd of 0.23 – remarkable for a four-door saloon. The ECC also needed to be identifiably a Volvo, so it had to draw on styling themes from previous cars – the Amazon's sides, the 144's broad shoulders and the V-shaped bonnet (hood), which had been a Volvo characteristic since the PV444, were all incorporated into the design.

SPECIFICATIONS

ENGINE CAPACITY:	n/a
CONFIGURATION:	front-mounted 42 kW (56 bhp) (gas turbine) plus 71 kW
POWER:	(95 bhp) (electric)
TOP SPEED:	175 km/h (109 mph)
TRANSMISSION:	two-speed auto, front-wheel drive
LENGTH:	4487 mm (176.65 in)
WIDTH:	1804 mm (71.02 in)
DEBUT:	Paris 1992

There was a gas turbine engine with an electric motor. The former was for high-speed use; the latter was for urban driving.

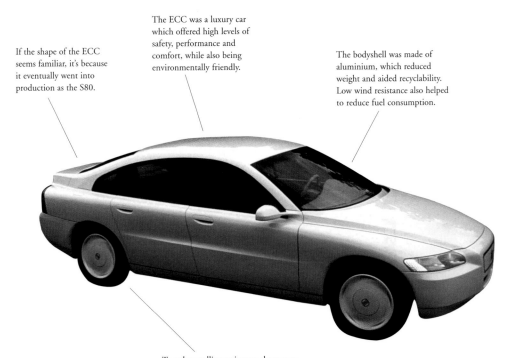

If the shape of the ECC seems familiar, it's because it eventually went into production as the S80.

The ECC was a luxury car which offered high levels of safety, performance and comfort, while also being environmentally friendly.

The bodyshell was made of aluminium, which reduced weight and aided recyclability. Low wind resistance also helped to reduce fuel consumption.

To reduce rolling resistance there were low-rolling-resistance tyres which were inflated to double the normal pressure.

FLIGHTS OF FANTASY

Perhaps one day some of these concepts won't be seen as especially revolutionary. Their designs and also the technologies they offer will be seen as mainstream. Already we're seeing some of the elements of the earlier designs making their way into affordable production cars – things such as flush glazing, satellite navigation, anti-lock brakes and glass roofs. While it is true that all of these concepts have one foot in the realms of fantasy, they're also not completely beyond the realms of possibility – it's just a question of making the sums add up. In some cases that means developing the technologies so they're more reliable or more affordable – but that time will come and once again the game will move on.

In many instances the cars could never be sold in their concept forms because of fundamental design elements; Saab would quickly be bankrupted if its Aero-X were offered for sale because of inherent safety flaws with the huge glass canopy. Meanwhile the Bertone Filo couldn't be sold because its drive-by-wire systems are illegal throughout Europe. But one day production processes and the laws will change, and car design will take another huge leap forward – just as it has done since the first cars of the late nineteenth century.

Left: *Beautiful and impressive – but a dead end in design terms. BMW's Mille Miglia was built purely to celebrate past glories.*

BERTONE KARISMA

Take a look at the Karisma and you'd be hard-pressed to guess which car donated its mechanicals to this 1994 show stopper. If you'd worked out it was the Porsche 911 you'd be doing pretty well – not least of all because the 911 is a car that's very rarely chosen as the basis for a concept, thanks to its rear-mounted engine. This wasn't the first time Bertone had rebodied a 911; in 1966 it attempted a similar exercise with its Roadster. While that car was a sports car, the Karisma was a four-seater saloon that was supposed to be fast yet practical.

SPECIFICATIONS

ENGINE CAPACITY: 3.6 litres
CONFIGURATION: rear-mounted flat-six
POWER: 186 kW (250 bhp)
TOP SPEED: 241 km/h (150 mph)
TRANSMISSION: rear-wheel drive
LENGTH: 4520 mm (177.95 in)
WIDTH: 1860 mm (73.23 in)
DEBUT: Geneva 1994

The whole of each side of the Karisma opened up via a single gullwing door, to reveal four seats and a lack of central pillars.

The exterior was characterized by large expanses of glass, in a bid to open up the interior as much as possible.

The interior was designed in such a way as to be completely uncluttered. That's why there was no central console.

Despite there being space for four occupants, luggage space was at a premium thanks to the engine taking up all of the rear.

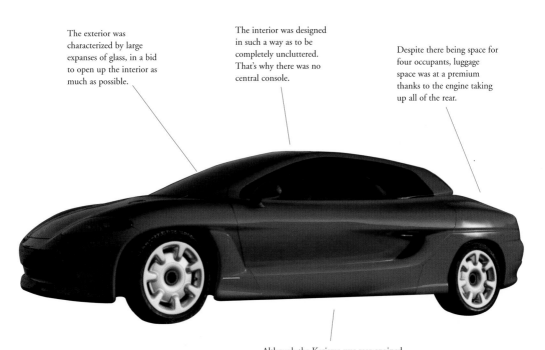

Although the Karisma was rear-engined and a spacious four-seater, it was no longer than a conventional family saloon.

BERTONE NIVOLA

U sing a Chevrolet Corvette engine, the Nivola was named after legendary racing driver Tazio Nuvolari and was Bertone's eighteenth mid-engined roadster. Looking similar to the Lamborghini-based Athon of a decade earlier, the Nivola featured a one-piece metal roof which could easily be removed, then slid under the engine cover for storage. While the major mechanicals were American, the chassis (along with pretty much the whole of the rest of the car) was completely Italian, complete with active suspension, 432-mm (17-in) OZ alloy wheels, ventilated discs all round and anti-lock brakes. The transmission was also engineered in Italy, with a five-ratio gearbox in place of the Corvette's usual six-speeder.

SPECIFICATIONS

ENGINE CAPACITY:	5727 cc
CONFIGURATION:	mid-mounted V8
POWER:	283 kW (380 bhp)
TOP SPEED:	306 km/h (190 mph)
TRANSMISSION:	five-speed manual, rear-wheel drive
LENGTH:	4204 mm (165.51 in)
WIDTH:	1981 mm (77.99 in)
DEBUT:	Geneva 1990

The Nivola's headlights weren't faired in; instead they were pop-up units that featured a pair of elliptical lenses on each side.

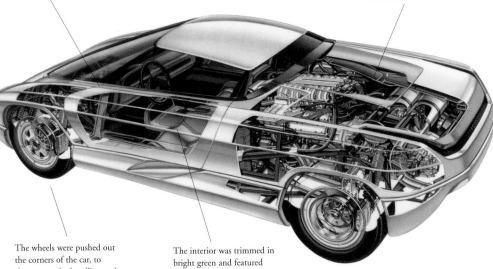

There was no luggage space in the front or rear; all bags were loaded into the doors, which were like panniers.

Massive performance was guaranteed, thanks to the use of a Chevrolet Corvette V8 engine, mounted behind the cabin.

The wheels were pushed out the corners of the car, to sharpen up the handling and improve the ride.

The interior was trimmed in bright green and featured electrically adjustable seats complete with a massage function.

BERTONE FILO

It may look futuristic from the outside, but it's not until you climb into the cabin that you realize just how advanced the Filo was. In fact it was so cutting edge that the car could be driven only on private roads. The reason for this was its drive-by-wire technology where all the major controls such as the brakes and steering were controlled entirely by electronics – something that was illegal throughout Europe. With just 0.1 turns from lock to lock, the steering took some getting used to, but using such technology meant the whole of the cabin could be opened right up by dispensing with the mechanical linkages.

SPECIFICATIONS

ENGINE CAPACITY:	1.8 litres
CONFIGURATION:	front-mounted four-cylinder petrol
POWER:	n/a
TOP SPEED:	n/a
TRANSMISSION:	five-speed manual, front-wheel drive
LENGTH:	n/a
WIDTH:	n/a
DEBUT:	Geneva 2001

The Filo may have looked minimalist, but there were 21 speakers scattered around the interior, complete with five-channel audio.

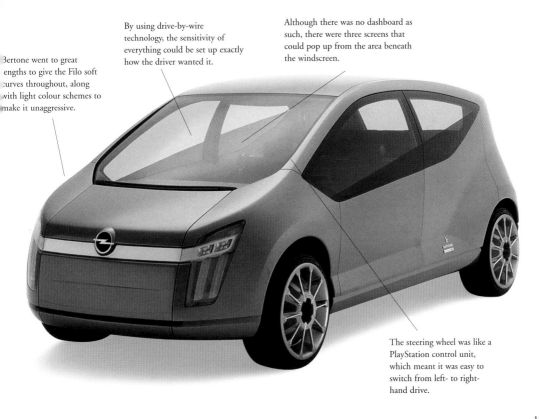

Bertone went to great lengths to give the Filo soft curves throughout, along with light colour schemes to make it unaggressive.

By using drive-by-wire technology, the sensitivity of everything could be set up exactly how the driver wanted it.

Although there was no dashboard as such, there were three screens that could pop up from the area beneath the windscreen.

The steering wheel was like a PlayStation control unit, which meant it was easy to switch from left- to right-hand drive.

BMW MILLE MIGLIA

It didn't take a genius to work out what the Mille Miglia concept was all about; as the name suggested, BMW created it in an attempt to congratulate itself on past glories. Having won the Mille Miglia way back in 1940 with the 328 Coupé – which averaged an incredible 167 km/h (104 mph) over 1600 km (1000 miles) – BMW decided to commemorate the victory 66 years later with a rebodied Z4M Coupé that echoed the lines of the victorious racer. Using modern design and construction methods, this concept married old and new techniques to superb effect, with the car being presented at the 2006 Mille Miglia.

SPECIFICATIONS

ENGINE CAPACITY:	3246 cc
CONFIGURATION:	front-mounted in-line six
POWER:	256 kW (343 bhp)
TOP SPEED:	249 km/h (155 mph) (limited)
TRANSMISSION:	six-speed manual, rear-wheel drive
LENGTH:	4343 mm (170.98 in)
WIDTH:	1904 mm (74.96 in)
DEBUT:	Mille Miglia 2006

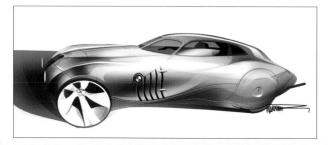

The lines of the Mille Miglia may have been retro, but those 508-mm (20-in) wheels and 245/40 R20 tyres were utterly contemporary.

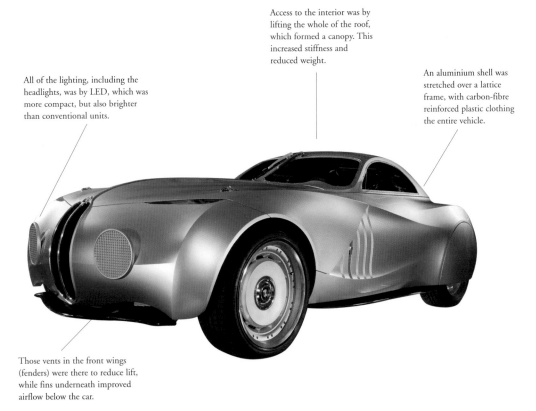

Access to the interior was by lifting the whole of the roof, which formed a canopy. This increased stiffness and reduced weight.

An aluminium shell was stretched over a lattice frame, with carbon-fibre reinforced plastic clothing the entire vehicle.

All of the lighting, including the headlights, was by LED, which was more compact, but also brighter than conventional units.

Those vents in the front wings (fenders) were there to reduce lift, while fins underneath improved airflow below the car.

BMW XCOUPÉ

If flame surfacing sounded like the sort of thing you could expect at the local Burger King, BMW designer Chris Bangle proved otherwise. However, while the burger joint's wares might be seen as quite tasty by some, there were few takers for Bangle's efforts; the xCoupé didn't go down very well. It wasn't just the lines that jarred; the lack of symmetry didn't help. One example of this was a pair of rear lights that differed from one side to the other, while there were also varying treatments of the pillars. However, while the xCoupé shocked, many elements of its design made it into BMW's production cars.

SPECIFICATIONS

ENGINE CAPACITY:	2926 cc turbocharged
CONFIGURATION:	front-mounted in-line six diesel
POWER:	137 kW (184 bhp)
TOP SPEED:	201 km/h (125 mph)
TRANSMISSION:	five-speed auto, four-wheel drive
LENGTH:	n/a
WIDTH:	n/a
DEBUT:	Detroit 2001

All four wheels of the xCoupé were driven, while the transmission was a five-speed automatic unit with sequential manual option.

The headlights swivelled with the front wheels to light the car's way – it was controlled by GPS rather than the steering.

Few concepts were fitted with diesel engines, but the xCoupé bucked this trend with its front-mounted six-cylinder unit.

A rear spoiler popped up at 110 km/h (68 mph) to maintain stability at high speeds, while the headlights turned with the front wheels.

Xcoupé

Monster 508-mm (20-in) alloy wheels were fitted, but with higher profile tyres than usual. They also featured run-flat technology.

187

CADILLAC IMAJ

While European cars have often sold very well in the United States, the Americans generally haven't done so well with their cars in Europe. The Imaj was supposed to change all that, which is why it wasn't even designed in America – its lines were penned in England. Despite this, the Imaj was still faithful to its American roots, thanks to its supercharged V8 engine and generous dimensions; few cars hailing from Europe measured over five metres (16 ft) in length at the time. While the Imaj itself didn't reach production, Cadillac had the courage of its convictions to use many of the styling cues in its production cars.

SPECIFICATIONS

ENGINE CAPACITY:	4228 cc supercharged
CONFIGURATION:	front-mounted petrol V8
POWER:	317 kW (425 bhp)
TOP SPEED:	249 km/h (155 mph)
TRANSMISSION:	five-speed auto, four-wheel drive
LENGTH:	5105 mm (200.98 in)
WIDTH:	1905 mm (75.00 in)
DEBUT:	Geneva 2000
DESIGNER:	Simon Cox

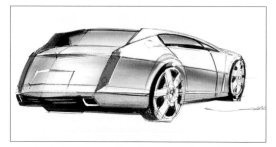

Being an American car, the Imaj had to be fitted with an automatic gearbox – in this case a five-speed unit feeding all four wheels.

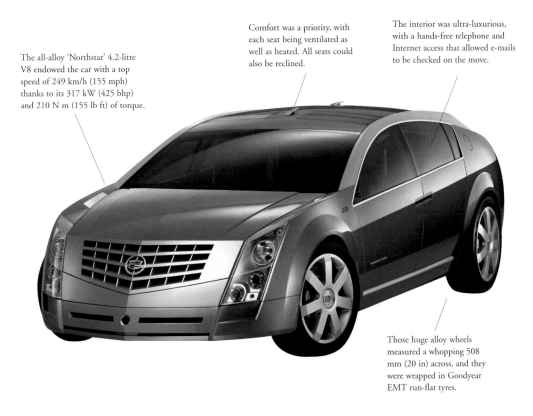

The all-alloy 'Northstar' 4.2-litre V8 endowed the car with a top speed of 249 km/h (155 mph) thanks to its 317 kW (425 bhp) and 210 N m (155 lb ft) of torque.

Comfort was a priority, with each seat being ventilated as well as heated. All seats could also be reclined.

The interior was ultra-luxurious, with a hands-free telephone and Internet access that allowed e-mails to be checked on the move.

Those huge alloy wheels measured a whopping 508 mm (20 in) across, and they were wrapped in Goodyear EMT run-flat tyres.

CHRYSLER IMPERIAL

The Imperial could almost have gone into the production cars chapter because it entered showrooms as the Rolls-Royce Phantom – except the Phantom went on sale before the Chrysler was first shown. When the covers were taken off the Imperial at the 2006 Detroit motor show, Chrysler claimed that the classic production models of the 1930s and 1950s that bore the same name had inspired its lines. You didn't have to look too hard, however, to see that it bore a much closer resemblance to the sole product of Rolls-Royce. All it needed was a Spirit of Ecstasy on the radiator grille and the effect would have been complete.

SPECIFICATIONS

ENGINE CAPACITY:	5.7 litres
CONFIGURATION:	front-mounted petrol V8
POWER:	254 kW (340 bhp)
TOP SPEED:	257 km/h (160 mph)
TRANSMISSION:	five-speed auto, rear-wheel drive
LENGTH:	5439 mm (214.13 in)
WIDTH:	1933 mm (76.10 in)
DEBUT:	Detroit 2006

Unsurprisingly, the interior of the Imperial was lavishly trimmed with cream and brown leather, accompanied by walnut trim.

Powering the Imperial was Chrysler's legendary Hemi, in 5.7-litre form. This produced 529 N m (390 lb ft) of torque to give zero to 97 km/h (60 mph) in 5.5 seconds.

The interior was amazingly spacious, thanks to a 3123-mm (122.95-in) wheelbase and a rather generous length of 5439 mm (214.13 in).

Lighting was state-of-the-art, with projector units up front; all of the rear illumination was taken care of by a series of LEDs.

Those massive alloy wheels are 559 mm (22 in) in diameter – which just happened to be the same size as a Rolls-Royce Phantom's …

CLARION C-AVCC

While concept cars are usually the preserve of car makers or design houses, occasionally a components manufacturer builds one to show off its wares. That was the case for Japan's largest car stereo manufacturer Clarion, which wheeled out the C-AVCC in 1986. The name was short for Car Audio, Visual, Computer and Communication, a snappy title that summed up what the car was all about – computer technology. It also summed up a peculiarly Japanese obsession – that of creating an abbreviation for everything to the point where this car featured CRT, SAW, PCM, RDS and PRS – among many more!

SPECIFICATIONS

ENGINE CAPACITY:	none fitted
CONFIGURATION:	mid-mounted
POWER:	non-runner
TOP SPEED:	n/a
TRANSMISSION:	rear-wheel drive
LENGTH:	n/a
WIDTH:	n/a
DEBUT:	Birmingham 1986
DESIGNER:	Takuya Yura

One look at the interior made it instantly clear when this car was built; those LED displays have dated, even if the exterior design hasn't.

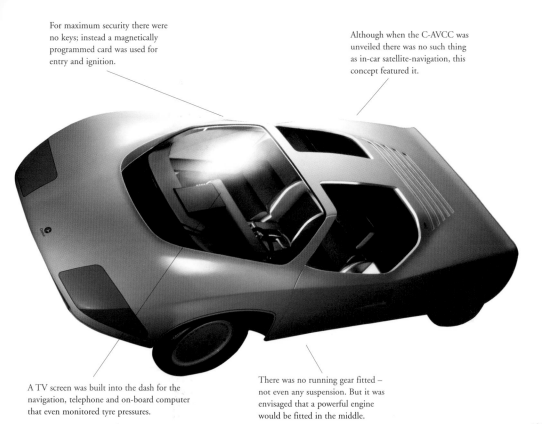

For maximum security there were no keys; instead a magnetically programmed card was used for entry and ignition.

Although when the C-AVCC was unveiled there was no such thing as in-car satellite-navigation, this concept featured it.

A TV screen was built into the dash for the navigation, telephone and on-board computer that even monitored tyre pressures.

There was no running gear fitted – not even any suspension. But it was envisaged that a powerful engine would be fitted in the middle.

FIORAVANTI VOLA

It was easy to see that the Vola was based on the Alfa Romeo GTV; this was the Italian design house's interpretation of what an Alfa Romeo of the future might look like. While the overall shape wasn't especially adventurous, the roof design was particularly neat, as it was a hard top which could literally be flipped over in seconds to open the car's interior targa-style. Folding hard tops were becoming very popular by the time of the Vola's arrival in 2001, but they were all much bulkier and less space efficient than the solution devised by Fioravanti; in fact, it was so good that Ferrari used it on the 575M Superamerica.

SPECIFICATIONS

ENGINE CAPACITY:	2959 cc
CONFIGURATION:	front-mounted V6 petrol
POWER:	163 kW (218 bhp)
TOP SPEED:	n/a
TRANSMISSION:	rear-wheel drive
LENGTH:	4160 mm (163.78 in)
WIDTH:	1810 mm (71.26 in)
DEBUT:	Geneva 2001

The most impressive aspect of the Vola was its folding roof, which simply flipped through 180 degrees.

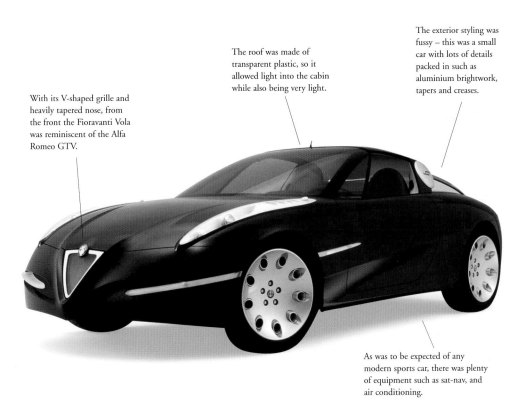

With its V-shaped grille and heavily tapered nose, from the front the Fioravanti Vola was reminiscent of the Alfa Romeo GTV.

The roof was made of transparent plastic, so it allowed light into the cabin while also being very light.

The exterior styling was fussy – this was a small car with lots of details packed in such as aluminium brightwork, tapers and creases.

As was to be expected of any modern sports car, there was plenty of equipment such as sat-nav, and air conditioning.

FORD PROBE IV

You're looking at the slipperiest car in the world – or at least that was the Probe IV's claim to fame when it arrived in 1983. As the name suggests, this was the fourth Probe concept in a series of five, while its predecessor eventually became the Sierra (in toned-down form). With a CD of 0.15, the Probe IV was incredibly slippery; it also incorporated a suspension system that adjusted the car's height depending on road speed. At high velocities the car sat just 10 cm (four inches) from the ground, but as the speed dropped it could be raised by several inches.

SPECIFICATIONS

ENGINE CAPACITY:	1.6 litres
CONFIGURATION:	front-mounted in-line four-cylinder petrol
POWER:	76 kW (102 bhp)
TOP SPEED:	n/a
TRANSMISSION:	three-speed auto, front-wheel drive
LENGTH:	4755 mm (187.20 in)
WIDTH:	1826 mm (71.89 in)
DEBUT:	Geneva 1983

So that the bonnet (hood) line could be kept as low as possible, the Probe IV's engine had to be canted over by 70 degrees.

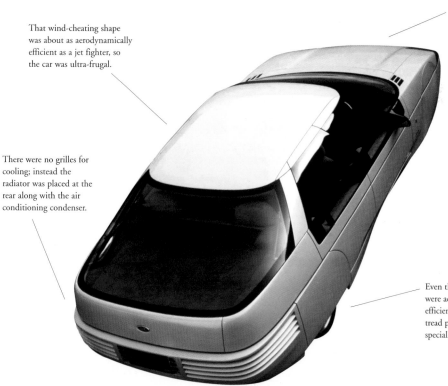

That wind-cheating shape was about as aerodynamically efficient as a jet fighter, so the car was ultra-frugal.

The air dam at the front was automatically adjusted for rake and angle depending on how fast the car was travelling.

There were no grilles for cooling; instead the radiator was placed at the rear along with the air conditioning condenser.

Even the wheels and tyres were aerodynamically efficient, with a slippery tread pattern developed specially by Goodyear.

HOLDEN EFIJY

I n the first few years of the twenty-first century, there was a battle between America's Big Three (GM, Ford and Chrysler) to see who could come up with the most retro concept car. While icons from the 1960s were frequently revived, Holden in Australia went back further and brought out this wild concept inspired by its FJ of the 1950s. While the lines of the car were distinctly post-war, the technology under the skin was twenty-first century. Based on a redundant Chevrolet Corvette C5 and with a 481-kW (645-bhp) supercharged V8, the EFIJY nearly didn't happen – it was started in 2001, but wasn't finished until 2005 because of cash shortages.

SPECIFICATIONS

ENGINE CAPACITY:	5665 cc
CONFIGURATION:	front-mounted V8
POWER:	481 kW (645 bhp)
TOP SPEED:	n/a
TRANSMISSION:	four-speed auto, rear-wheel drive
LENGTH:	5162 mm (203.23 in)
WIDTH:	1999 mm (78.70 in)
DEBUT:	Sydney 2005
DESIGNER:	Richard Ferlazzo

The key stylistic links between the EFIJY and the FJ that inspired it were the grille, wings (fenders), bonnet (hood) and torpedo rear wings.

The air suspension was capable of lowering the car to sit just 27 mm (1.06 in) above the ground – or it could be raised to 139 mm (5.47 in).

Every single light in the car was an LED rather than a bulb, while there was a touch-screen display on the dash.

Those monster alloy wheels measured 508 mm (20 in) across at the front – the ones at the rear were another 51 mm (two inches) in diameter!

The Corvette's rolling chassis was lengthened to accommodate the EFIJY body, which is over 700 mm (27.56 in) longer than the FJ which inspired it.

HYUNDAI HCD-I

If only Hyundai could serve up a few production vehicles that looked as exciting as the HCD-1, the company would surely enjoy a massive image boost. While its production vehicles are invariably devoid of any kind of excitement, the HCD-I proved that Hyundai's designers were capable of injecting some emotion into their cars. The first fruit of Hyundai's California Design Centre, the HCD-I was a serious proposal for a production car from the usually highly conservative Korean car maker. It was meant to be on sale by 1995, at a cost of just $14,000 – but the project seems to have stalled somewhere …

SPECIFICATIONS

ENGINE CAPACITY:	1997 cc
CONFIGURATION:	front-mounted in-line four-cylinder petrol
POWER:	112 kW (150 bhp)
TOP SPEED:	n/a
TRANSMISSION:	front-wheel drive
LENGTH:	3927 mm (154.61 in)
WIDTH:	1732 mm (68.19 in)
DEBUT:	Detroit 1992

This was a cheap sports car, but there was still plenty of kit such as airbags, hi-fi and disc brakes front and rear.

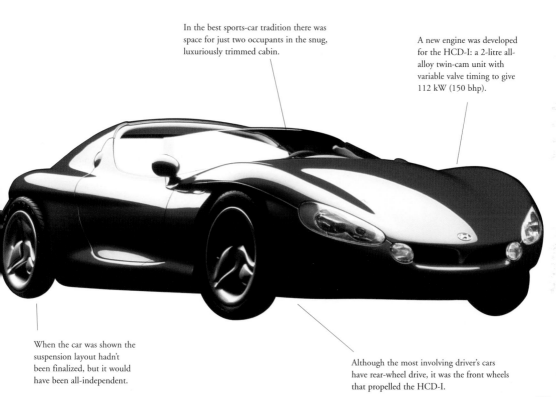

In the best sports-car tradition there was space for just two occupants in the snug, luxuriously trimmed cabin.

A new engine was developed for the HCD-I: a 2-litre all-alloy twin-cam unit with variable valve timing to give 112 kW (150 bhp).

When the car was shown the suspension layout hadn't been finalized, but it would have been all-independent.

Although the most involving driver's cars have rear-wheel drive, it was the front wheels that propelled the HCD-I.

HYUNDAI HCD-II

Aﬂer the positive reception the HCD-I enjoyed, it made sense for
Hyundai to follow up that concept with another, to show it wasn't
merely a flash in the pan. The result was the HCD-II, billed as a sports car
that was both stylish and practical; make up your own mind whether it really
had these attributes. Designed to compete with the Honda Prelude and
Nissan 200SX, the HCD-II had a 2.0-litre four-cylinder engine that pushed
its 112 kW (150 bhp) through the front wheels. There was plenty of
technology, with projector headlights, a collision avoidance system and
carbon-fibre panelling for the interior seats.

SPECIFICATIONS

ENGINE CAPACITY:	2000 cc
CONFIGURATION:	front-mounted in-line four
POWER:	112 kW (150 bhp)
TOP SPEED:	n/a
TRANSMISSION:	front-wheel drive
LENGTH:	4265 mm (167.91 in)
WIDTH:	1758 mm (69.21 in)
DEBUT:	Detroit 1993

*Unusually, there were two seats in the front of the
HCD-II, but just one in the back; the rear occupant
faced sideways.*

The 112-kW (150-bhp) 2.0-litre 16-valve powerplant in the nose was the first outing for Hyundai's all-new Beta unit.

To highlight the HCD-II's sporty pretensions there was a long bonnet (hood) and the three-seater cabin was set well back.

With this car, Hyundai was attempting to offer a muscular, aggressive car with those broad shoulders and pinched mid-section.

Access to the single rear seat was by the passenger door only, which was longer than the one on the driver's side.

ISUZU ZEN

The ZEN neatly mixed the rugged spirit of a sport utility vehicle, the functionality of a commercial vehicle and the stolid demeanour of a traditional Japanese tatami room. Its maker, Isuzu, claimed that the major design themes for the vehicle were Japan's ancient essence of harmony and interior volume enclosed by geometric lines that echo modern architecture. It built on the success of the Kai concept that had been seen at the same show two years earlier, but it wasn't designed in Japan. Instead, it was created in England and inspired by a visit to the modern art on display at the Tate Gallery in London – hence the disjointed lines.

SPECIFICATIONS

ENGINE CAPACITY:	3 litres
CONFIGURATION:	front-mounted turbodiesel V6
POWER:	n/a
TOP SPEED:	n/a
TRANSMISSION:	four-speed automatic, four-wheel drive
LENGTH:	n/a
WIDTH:	n/a
DEBUT:	Tokyo 2001
DESIGNER:	Geoffrey Gardiner

The design featured three distinct zones: the engine bay, the passenger compartment and the van-like load bay.

There was independent double-wishbone suspension up front and a rigid rear axle supported by leaf springs at the rear.

The digital instrument panel was positioned in a thin, horizontal space near the base of the windscreen.

Isuzu fitted its 3.0-litre V6 turbodiesel into that stubby nose, which drove all four wheels via an automatic gearbox.

Riding on 508-mm (20-in) wheels all round, the 225/65R-20 run-flat tyres were designed and produced specially by Bridgestone.

205

ITALDESIGN MORAY

The Corvette celebrated its fiftieth anniversary in 2003, so it was only fitting that the occasion was marked with one or two tributes. One of these came from Giorgetto and Fabrizio Giugaro at Italdesign, who wished to pay homage to what was America's most enduring sports-car brand – and almost certainly the most highly respected. Immersing themselves in marketing hype as only car designers can, this concept was 'designed as though touched by drifting tides with long and slender front lights, bringing immediately to the mind the moray, the English term for the eel-type fish'. It may have been a pseudy explanation, but the lines were fabulous.

SPECIFICATIONS

ENGINE CAPACITY:	6 litres
CONFIGURATION:	front-mounted V8 petrol
POWER:	298 kW (400 bhp)
TOP SPEED:	n/a
TRANSMISSION:	four-speed auto, rear-wheel drive
LENGTH:	4540 mm (178.74 in)
WIDTH:	1950 mm (76.77 in)
DEBUT:	Geneva 2003

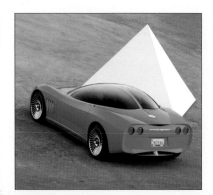

To keep the lines of the Moray as clean as possible there were no external mirrors – instead there was a camera in the rear panel.

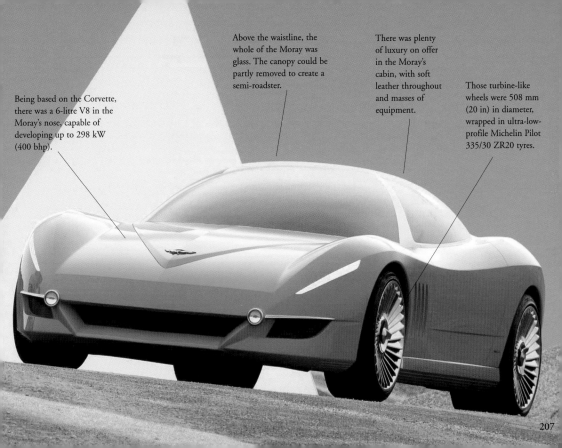

Being based on the Corvette, there was a 6-litre V8 in the Moray's nose, capable of developing up to 298 kW (400 bhp).

Above the waistline, the whole of the Moray was glass. The canopy could be partly removed to create a semi-roadster.

There was plenty of luxury on offer in the Moray's cabin, with soft leather throughout and masses of equipment.

Those turbine-like wheels were 508 mm (20 in) in diameter, wrapped in ultra-low-profile Michelin Pilot 335/30 ZR20 tyres.

ITALDESIGN NAZCA C2 SPIDER

The Nazca that was unveiled at the 1991 Geneva motor show was the first of three. First there was the Nazca M12, followed by the Nazca C2, which arrived later that year at the Tokyo motor show. Finally, in 1993, came what was perhaps the most dramatic of the trio – the Nazca C2 Spider. All were fantastic-looking supercars with amazing road presence and hugely powerful engines – but none of them made that leap to production status, as had originally been hoped. Perhaps if the global recession hadn't hit just at that time things would have been different, but, as it was, the Nazca was relegated to museum-exhibit status.

SPECIFICATIONS

ENGINE CAPACITY:	4988 cc
CONFIGURATION:	mid-mounted V12 petrol
POWER:	224 kW (300 bhp)
TOP SPEED:	298 km/h (185 mph)
TRANSMISSION:	five-speed manual, rear-wheel drive
LENGTH:	4365 mm (171.85 in)
WIDTH:	1990 mm (78.35 in)
DEBUT:	Geneva 1991

This is the final Nazca of the trio produced; it featured a bigger engine than the first car and was the only open-topped concept of the three.

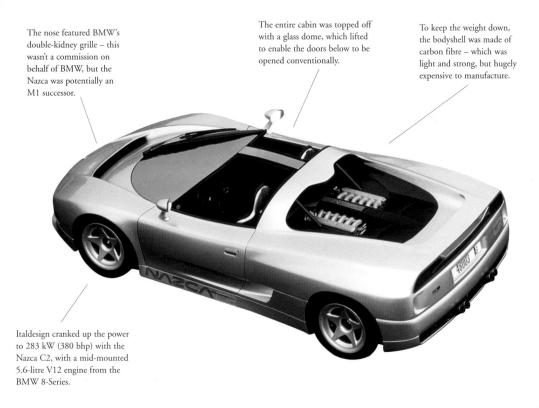

The nose featured BMW's double-kidney grille – this wasn't a commission on behalf of BMW, but the Nazca was potentially an M1 successor.

The entire cabin was topped off with a glass dome, which lifted to enable the doors below to be opened conventionally.

To keep the weight down, the bodyshell was made of carbon fibre – which was light and strong, but hugely expensive to manufacture.

Italdesign cranked up the power to 283 kW (380 bhp) with the Nazca C2, with a mid-mounted 5.6-litre V12 engine from the BMW 8-Series.

JAGUAR R COUPE

It could come as no surprise that Jaguar was in financial trouble when it produced beautiful show cars such as the R Coupe, but then refused to offer them, instead selling safely designed vehicles such as the S-Type and XJ. If only the company would break its production cars free of the shackles of retro design and produce an R Coupe that its customers could buy, surely the tide would be turned? This is perhaps the best-looking car Jaguar has ever unveiled, and, while its second-generation XK is hardly a dog, it has to be said that the R Coupe has infinitely more presence. Perhaps soon Jaguar will learn the error of its ways.

SPECIFICATIONS

ENGINE CAPACITY:	3996 cc (proposed)
CONFIGURATION:	front-engined petrol V8
POWER:	276 kW (370 bhp)
TOP SPEED:	n/a
TRANSMISSION:	automatic, rear-wheel drive
LENGTH:	4925 mm (193.90 in)
WIDTH:	1890 mm (74.41 in)
DEBUT:	Frankfurt 2001
DESIGNER:	Ian Callum/Julian Thomson

The R Coupe concept wasn't a runner, but it featured an S-Type transmission and suspension; there was no engine fitted.

The twin fuel filler caps were silver plated, while the car's badges were made of solid pieces of silver.

The headlights were active, which meant they turned with the front wheels, lighting the way around corners.

The 10-spoke alloy wheels were 533 mm (21 in) in diameter. They were wrapped in amazingly low-profile 285/30 Continental tyres.

Most of the exterior lighting was by LED, with the stop lights glowing brighter, the harder the brake pedal was applied.

KARMANN SPORT UTILITY CABRIO

Car manufacturers have an aversion to building four-door convertibles, even as concept cars. Perhaps it's because such vehicles invariably have the structural integrity of a warm jelly, but whatever the reason it was clear that Karmann's Sport Utility Cabrio was never going to progress beyond the concept stage. Perhaps that wasn't so bad because it wasn't exactly good-looking, but it was fabulously engineered with its BMW-derived V8, fully functioning safety systems and electronic gadgetry galore which was all up and running. Designed and engineered in partnership with transmission specialist ZF, the SUC featured networked electronics that tied together all the car's systems for maximum reliability.

SPECIFICATIONS

ENGINE CAPACITY:	4401 cc
CONFIGURATION:	front-mounted petrol V8
POWER:	239 kW (320 bhp)
TOP SPEED:	n/a
TRANSMISSION:	six-speed auto, four-wheel drive
LENGTH:	4638 mm (182.60 in)
WIDTH:	2180 mm (85.83 in)
DEBUT:	Frankfurt 2005

The rear window was incorporated into the tailgate rather than the roof; it could then be easily retracted to ventilate the cabin when the roof was up.

Perhaps uniquely, the folding cloth roof (the world's largest powered roof) incorporated a glass sunroof in its leading edge.

Behind the rear seats there were two rollover bars that popped up automatically if the sensors detected the car was going to invert.

Safety was paramount, with crash energy being dissipated throughout the car's structure in the event of a collision.

Rear-hinged back doors were coming back into fashion – but having no central pillar on a convertible was asking for trouble.

213

LAMBORGHINI ATHON

There's a good chance that if Bertone hadn't created the Athon in 1980, Lamborghini would have disappeared for ever. The company was in dire straits, and the Athon raised its profile to the point where the company was worth saving. Based on the Silhouette, the Athon was for sunny climes only, as there was no provision for any kind of weather protection, except for the windscreen. With no roof of any kind, the space behind the cabin could be given over entirely to the engine.

SPECIFICATIONS

ENGINE CAPACITY:	2996 cc
CONFIGURATION:	mid-mounted V8
POWER:	198 kW (265 bhp)
TOP SPEED:	259 km/h (161 mph)
TRANSMISSION:	five-speed manual, rear-wheel drive
LENGTH:	3970 mm (156.30 in)
WIDTH:	1888 mm (74.33 in)
DEBUT:	Turin 1980
DESIGNER:	Marc Deschamps

While the car still looks fresh on the outside, it's dated by its interior, which is dominated by the electronic displays. With LCDs and LEDs just coming into fashion, concept cars of the time were invariably overloaded with them.

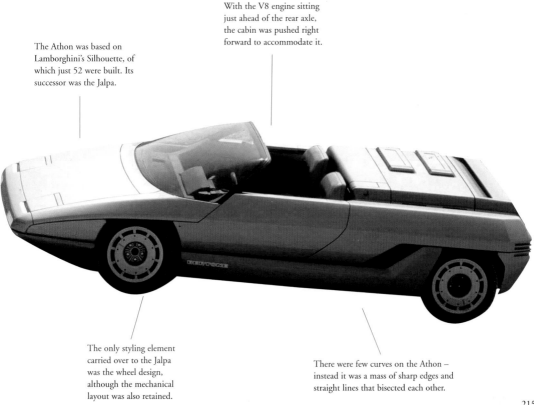

The Athon was based on Lamborghini's Silhouette, of which just 52 were built. Its successor was the Jalpa.

With the V8 engine sitting just ahead of the rear axle, the cabin was pushed right forward to accommodate it.

The only styling element carried over to the Jalpa was the wheel design, although the mechanical layout was also retained.

There were few curves on the Athon – instead it was a mass of sharp edges and straight lines that bisected each other.

215

LINCOLN NAVICROSS

It may look like a large, luxury saloon, but the Navicross was much more than that. Designed to be a sporty alternative to a full-blown sport utility vehicle, this showstopper was first seen at the 2003 Detroit motor show. After the appearance of the sinister-looking Lincoln Sentinel at the same event seven years earlier, it was clear that Ford's upmarket US division was set to take a new design direction. Although American cars hadn't been especially curvaceous since the 1950s, these new cars were taking the hard edges to extremes – standing too close to either the Sentinel or the Navicross, there was a good chance you'd cut yourself.

SPECIFICATIONS

ENGINE CAPACITY:	4.2 litres
CONFIGURATION:	front-mounted V8
	supercharged
POWER:	n/a
TOP SPEED:	n/a
TRANSMISSION:	five-speed semiauto,
	four-wheel drive
LENGTH:	4741 mm (186.6 in)
WIDTH:	1862 mm (73.31 in)
DEBUT:	Detroit 2003
DESIGNER:	Gerry McGovern

The leather-lined cabin was opened up with the adoption of rear-hinged back doors. There was seating for four – in true luxury.

With a 4.2-litre V8, the Navicross wouldn't have been wanting for power. It was also torquey, which was perfect for off-roading.

The raised ride height gave much-improved off-roading capabilities, along with compromised on-road performance, due to the higher centre of gravity.

The sweeping swage line gave the Navicross great confidence; it went from the car's nose to the bottom of the tail panel.

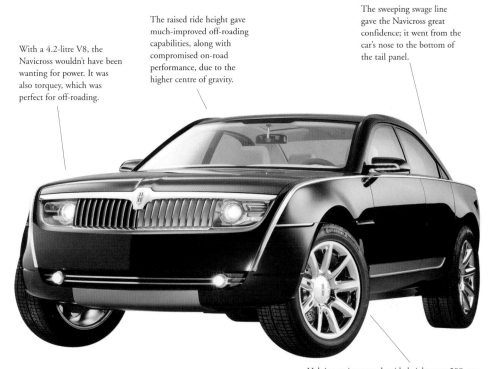

Helping to increase the ride height were 508-mm (20-in) alloy wheels. The short overhangs front and rear also helped when off-roading.

MAZDA RX-01

When you consider that the covers were first taken off this car in 1995, it still looks amazingly fresh. The RX-01 was developed as a potential successor to the RX-7. Smaller and lighter than the third-generation RX-7, the RX-01 featured a normally aspirated twin-rotor powerplant. Thanks to its compact dimensions it could be set well back in the chassis to improve the dynamics – yet it was still powerful enough to take the car to 97 km/h (60 mph) in under six seconds. The RX-8 may look great – but think how much better it would have been if this car had gone on sale.

SPECIFICATIONS

ENGINE CAPACITY: 654 cc x 2
CONFIGURATION: front-mounted rotary
POWER: 164 kW (220 bhp)
TOP SPEED: n/a
TRANSMISSION: five-speed manual, rear-wheel drive
LENGTH: 4054 mm (159.61 in)
WIDTH: 1730 mm (68.11 in)
DEBUT: Tokyo 1995

Those ultra-slim headlights were possible thanks to the use of LED technology. The low bonnet (hood) line was thanks to the rotary engine.

There was still a rotary engine tucked away in the nose, but there were no turbochargers. The result was 164 kW (220 bhp).

Using a small engine meant that it could be positioned down and back in the chassis to improve handling significantly.

You'd never believe it, but the RX-01 was a four-seater. The rear seats were useless for anyone with legs, though.

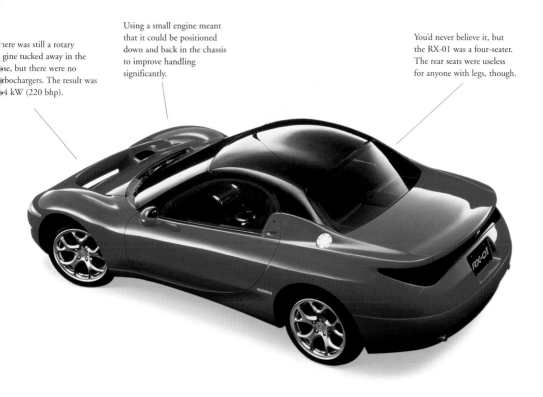

MINI SPIRITUAL

It was no secret in spring 1997 that there was an all-new Mini on the way. With the original Mini nearly four decades old, a new solution was needed to address the problem of urban motoring. The thing was that this car didn't represent the required solution, despite the fact that this was a concept from the Mini stable – or more accurately, a pair of concepts. There was the Spiritual, which was the two-door car, while the Spiritual Too offered a quartet of doors. Taking up no more road space than the original Mini, the Spiritual was much more spacious inside – but in the event the new Mini was even bigger.

SPECIFICATIONS

ENGINE CAPACITY:	800cc
CONFIGURATION:	rear-mounted three-cylinder petrol
POWER:	45 kW (60 bhp)
TOP SPEED:	161 km/h (100 mph)
TRANSMISSION:	rear-wheel drive
LENGTH:	3048 mm (120.00 in)
WIDTH:	n/a
DEBUT:	Geneva 1997

Although the Spiritual Too (left) was barely longer than a Fiat Punto, it offered more cabin space than a Mercedes S-Class.

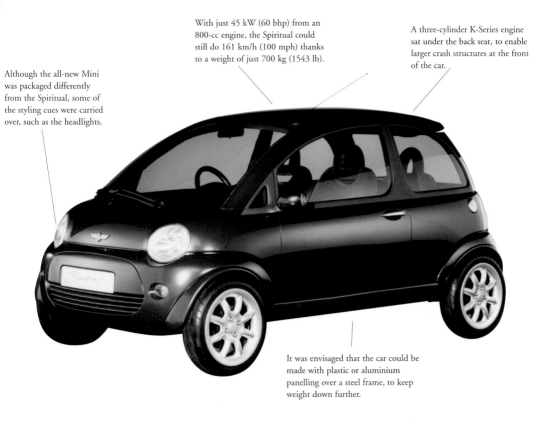

Although the all-new Mini was packaged differently from the Spiritual, some of the styling cues were carried over, such as the headlights.

With just 45 kW (60 bhp) from an 800-cc engine, the Spiritual could still do 161 km/h (100 mph) thanks to a weight of just 700 kg (1543 lb).

A three-cylinder K-Series engine sat under the back seat, to enable larger crash structures at the front of the car.

It was envisaged that the car could be made with plastic or aluminium panelling over a steel frame, to keep weight down further.

MITSUBISHI SUP

Designed for 'free-thinkers in the Internet society' the SUP, or Sports Utility Pack, attempted to be all things to all people by combining as many sectors as possible. There was a bit of MPV in there, along with some family car, sports car and a healthy dose of convertible. If only the design had been more coherent the whole thing may have made some sense, but it looked as if it had melted in the sun. Still, there was no denying the SUP looked modern – Mitsubishi was heading into deep financial trouble when it was unveiled, so something was needed to save the day. Unfortunately for Mitsubishi, the SUP wasn't it.

SPECIFICATIONS

ENGINE CAPACITY:	1999 cc
CONFIGURATION:	front-mounted four-
POWER:	cylinder petrol
	n/a
TOP SPEED:	n/a
TRANSMISSION:	automatic, part-time
	four-wheel drive
LENGTH:	4166 mm (164.02 in)
WIDTH:	1854 mm (72.99 in)
DEBUT:	Frankfurt 2001

The SUP had a bizarre shower attachment which was accessed from a panel in the wing.

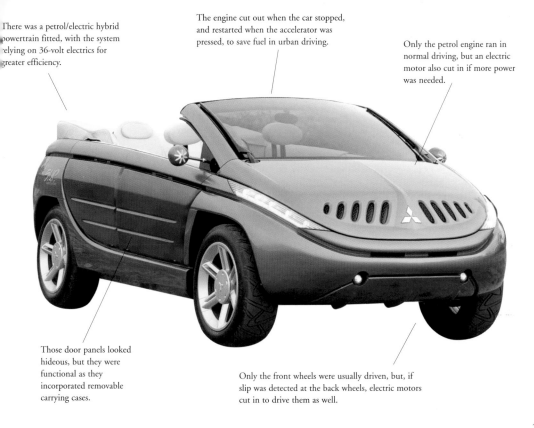

There was a petrol/electric hybrid powertrain fitted, with the system relying on 36-volt electrics for greater efficiency.

The engine cut out when the car stopped, and restarted when the accelerator was pressed, to save fuel in urban driving.

Only the petrol engine ran in normal driving, but an electric motor also cut in if more power was needed.

Those door panels looked hideous, but they were functional as they incorporated removable carrying cases.

Only the front wheels were usually driven, but, if slip was detected at the back wheels, electric motors cut in to drive them as well.

NISSAN DUNEHAWK

U ntil the arrival of the Volvo XC90, there wasn't a sport utility vehicle (SUV) which also offered proper seating for seven – Nissan decided to exploit that with the Dunehawk. Whereas Volvo had chosen not to turn its contender into a proper off-roader, Nissan went the whole nine yards to create a machine that was as capable as anything to come out of the gates of Land Rover. More intriguingly, it was also claimed that the Dunehawk pointed the way for the company's off-roaders of the future – the X-Trail had shown that Nissan wasn't afraid to style its off-roaders boldly and aggressively.

SPECIFICATIONS

ENGINE CAPACITY:	3501 cc
CONFIGURATION:	front-engined V6
POWER:	209 kW (280 bhp)
TOP SPEED:	n/a
TRANSMISSION:	five-speed automatic, four-wheel drive
LENGTH:	4795 mm (188.78 in)
WIDTH:	1900 mm (74.80 in)
DEBUT:	Frankfurt 2003

Flexibility and practicality were key inside. There were multiple seat configurations and masses of space behind the front seats.

The Dunehawk combined the characteristics of both an MPV and an off-roader, so it was a go-anywhere people-carrier.

The Dunehawk was fitted with a separate chassis, which enabled it to venture into the wilds without fear of getting stuck.

Luxury was standard – there was a multimedia system along with electric adjustment of just about everything that moved.

To keep the Dunehawk moving, hill descent control, traction control, anti-lock brakes and electronic stability protection were all fitted.

OLDSMOBILE PROFILE

As the Profile was unveiled at the 2000 Detroit motor show, Oldsmobile's planning director Peter Kosak claimed that 'over the past three years, the company's management has redefined what the company is all about'. But it was too little too late – within four years Oldsmobile would be dead, having survived for over a century. The Profile was a last-ditch attempt to raise Oldsmobile's reputation, offering a vehicle that was a cross between a sporting estate (station wagon) and a multipurpose vehicle. And a good attempt it was, too, but simply not enough people aspired to own an Oldsmobile and the writing was on the wall.

SPECIFICATIONS

ENGINE CAPACITY:	3.5 litres supercharged
CONFIGURATION:	front-mounted petrol V6
POWER:	186 kW (250 bhp)
TOP SPEED:	n/a
TRANSMISSION:	four-speed auto, four-wheel drive
LENGTH:	4707 mm (185.31 in)
WIDTH:	1880 mm (74.02 in)
DEBUT:	Detroit 2000

The electronics were state of the art, with satellite navigation that linked into real-time travel news to divert if necessary.

Even with a supercharger fitted there was just 186 kW (250 bhp) available from the 3.5-litre V6 in the nose; there was also 353 N m (260 lb ft) of torque.

Each passenger had their own entertainment, with individual displays and headphones available for everyone.

For added safety all four wheels were driven, with the power being fed to them via a four-speed automatic transmission.

Accessibility was key, with front doors on extended hinges and rear doors that slid backwards to open in confined spaces.

PEUGEOT RC

The purpose of the RC concepts was to create a pair of sporting 2 + 2 coupés, while challenging the thinking that it was unacceptable to use an oil-burning engine for a car the main point of which was driving pleasure. That was why there were two concepts built – one petrol and the other diesel – so that direct comparisons could be made between them, proving for once and for all that the diesel-engined car was no longer the poor relation. Driving pleasure was the key to these cars, so they featured a mid-mounted engine. Light weight also played its part in making the RC concepts fun to drive, with carbon-fibre and honeycomb panels.

SPECIFICATIONS

ENGINE CAPACITY:	2168 cc
CONFIGURATION:	mid-mounted in-line four-cylinder diesel
POWER:	129 kW (173 bhp)
TOP SPEED:	230 km/h (143 mph)
TRANSMISSION:	six-speed manual, rear-wheel drive
LENGTH:	4300 mm (169.29 in)
WIDTH:	1800 mm (70.87 in)
DEBUT:	Geneva 2002
DESIGNER:	Nicolas Brissoneau

The interiors of both the petrol and diesel versions of the RC featured red and black leather, with lots of aluminium and stainless-steel highlights.

Of the two engines, the diesel promised the better drive because of its superior torque; the turbocharged 2.2-litre 'four' gave 400 N m (295 lb ft).

Despite the powerplants being mid-mounted, both of the RCs were four-seaters. But there wasn't much room in the back.

There were two RCs built: the red one (Diamonds) featured a diesel engine; the black one (Spades) had a petrol unit.

The front end featured typical Peugeot styling cues, most notably those teardrop-shaped headlights. More unusual were the heavily kinked A-pillars.

PEUGEOT FELINE

Taking the largest saloon car in the range and building a small, nimble sports car on its platform may seem like madness, but that's what Peugeot did when it based its Feline concept on the 607. The attraction of using such a large car was that the wheels could be pushed right out to the corners, for maximum agility without compromising ride quality. Also, by using the 3.0-litre V6 in such a small car, the power-to-weight ratio could be maximized; with a weight of just 875 kg (1929 lb) there was a healthy 179 kW (240 bhp) per tonne on offer. Sadly, while it looked fabulous, the car could never be engineered for series production.

SPECIFICATIONS

ENGINE CAPACITY:	2946 cc
CONFIGURATION:	front-mounted V6 petrol
POWER:	157 kW (210 bhp)
TOP SPEED:	n/a
TRANSMISSION:	five-speed manual, front-wheel drive
LENGTH:	4070 mm (160.24 in)
WIDTH:	1880 mm (74.02 in)
DEBUT:	Geneva 2000

That long bonnet (hood) hinted at a huge powerhouse below. Again, the Feline took this to extremes, despite its relatively small engine.

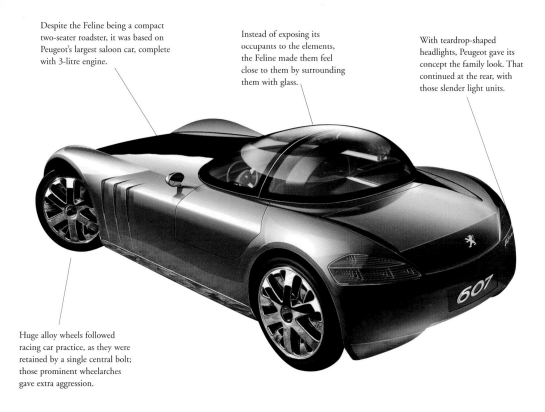

Despite the Feline being a compact two-seater roadster, it was based on Peugeot's largest saloon car, complete with 3-litre engine.

Instead of exposing its occupants to the elements, the Feline made them feel close to them by surrounding them with glass.

With teardrop-shaped headlights, Peugeot gave its concept the family look. That continued at the rear, with those slender light units.

Huge alloy wheels followed racing car practice, as they were retained by a single central bolt; those prominent wheelarches gave extra aggression.

PONTIAC SUNFIRE

Although the Pontiac Sunfire appeared as long ago as 1990, it wasn't until much more recently that American car design picked up to the point where it could seriously challenge the Europeans. Had the Sunfire – or a car like it – reached the showrooms, it would have upped the stakes somewhat and maybe provided a catalyst for more attractive US cars. It wasn't just the outside that was radical, though; the interior was just as cutting edge. The neatest aspect was the steering hub that remained static as the wheel was turned; this contained the instrumentation so it had to stay upright.

SPECIFICATIONS

ENGINE CAPACITY:	2400 cc
CONFIGURATION:	front-mounted in-line four-cylinder
POWER:	142 kW (190 bhp)
TOP SPEED:	n/a
TRANSMISSION:	five-speed manual, front-wheel drive
LENGTH:	n/a
WIDTH:	n/a
DEBUT:	Detroit 1990

The Sunfire went into production in toned-down form; there was also a Sunfire Speedster concept unveiled in 1994.

The whole of the upper half of the car was made of glass, for aerodynamics as well as for greater visibility.

Instead of being at the front of the car, the headlights were at the base of the windscreen. They rotated upwards for use.

It looked like a two-door car, but the Sunfire had four doors. The rear ones hinged backwards and there was no central pillar.

RENAULT RACOON

Think about all the successful amphibious vehicles that have been built over the years and you won't come up with a very long list. Reduce it to those offered for general sale and it'll be even shorter, so Renault's Racoon never made any sense from the outset. However, with a reputation for innovation, Renault was a company about which nobody ever said that its cars – and even less so its concepts – should ever be remotely rational. With hydrojets and a conventional petrol engine, the Racoon would certainly have been fun – but how Renault could have built it at anything like an affordable price was a problem that would never be solved.

SPECIFICATIONS

ENGINE CAPACITY:	2963 cc twin-turbo
CONFIGURATION:	rear-mounted petrol V6
POWER:	195 kW (262 bhp)
TOP SPEED:	156 km/h (97 mph)
TRANSMISSION:	six-speed manual, four-wheel drive
LENGTH:	n/a
WIDTH:	n/a
DEBUT:	Geneva 1993

The Racoon's styling was inspired by a helicopter cockpit, while the colour scheme reflected the animal after which the concept was named.

The twin-turbo V6 engine was borrowed from the Safrane and, mounted at the rear of the Racoon, it drove all four wheels.

There were huge expanses of photochromatic glass, with the windscreen chemically treated so it didn't need any wipers.

The suspension could be raised just on one side or end, so the cabin could remain level while driving on a slope.

There was usually 300 mm (11.81 in) of ground clearance, but when the Racoon was off-roading this could be increased to 500 mm (19.69 in).

SAAB EV-1

For a car maker as conservative as Saab, the EV-1 was a real break with tradition – if only the company had put it into production to shake off its staid image. But from the day the concept was unveiled, the Swedish car maker claimed it was just an engine and styling test bed – the EV-1 wouldn't reach the showroom. Although the EV-1 looked like a sports car, it was no more than a sporting 2 + 2. Saab had dabbled with sports-car production with its Sonett series of the 1960s, but alongside its more traditional family cars the Sonett made little impact – and Saab didn't want to go down that route again.

SPECIFICATIONS

ENGINE CAPACITY:	1985 cc
CONFIGURATION:	front-mounted in-line four petrol
POWER:	213 kW (285 bhp)
TOP SPEED:	270 km/h (168 mph)
TRANSMISSION:	front-wheel drive
LENGTH:	n/a
WIDTH:	n/a
DEBUT:	Los Angeles Auto Expo 1985
DESIGNER:	Bjorn Envall

The interior of the EV-1 was more restrained than the outside. The cabin featured seating for four, although the rear seats were a token gesture.

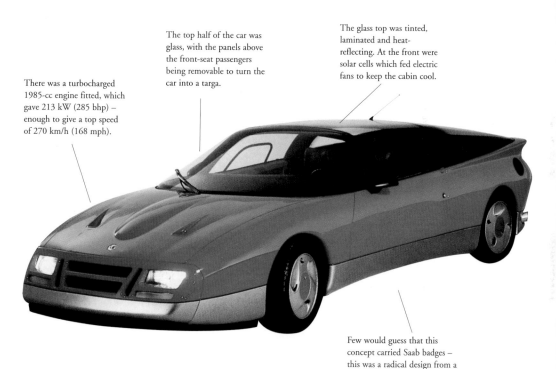

There was a turbocharged 1985-cc engine fitted, which gave 213 kW (285 bhp) – enough to give a top speed of 270 km/h (168 mph).

The top half of the car was glass, with the panels above the front-seat passengers being removable to turn the car into a targa.

The glass top was tinted, laminated and heat-reflecting. At the front were solar cells which fed electric fans to keep the cabin cool.

Few would guess that this concept carried Saab badges – this was a radical design from a very conservative company.

SAAB AERO-X

Car makers are notoriously poor at keeping secrets; one that was worth keeping was Saab's Aero-X, which made its surprise debut at the 2005 Geneva motor show. For a company that had pretty much disappeared from view to many, here was one of the best-looking cars ever designed, coming from a company producing cars that didn't appear to have been updated for years. While the Aero-X was never intended for production, it did show that General Motors was finally taking an interest in its Swedish outpost, which it had neglected for so long. At last there was hope that Saabs would be sexy …

SPECIFICATIONS

ENGINE CAPACITY:	2.8 litres twin-turbo
CONFIGURATION:	front-mounted bio-ethanol V6
POWER:	298 kW (400 bhp)
TOP SPEED:	249 km/h (155 mph)
TRANSMISSION:	seven-speed semiauto, four-wheel drive
LENGTH:	4675 mm (184.05 in)
WIDTH:	1918 mm (75.51 in)
DEBUT:	Geneva 2005
DESIGNER:	Anthony Lo, Alex Daniel, Erik Rokke

Instead of conventional doors, the Aero-X had a canopy that lifted up to expose the whole of the vehicle's interior.

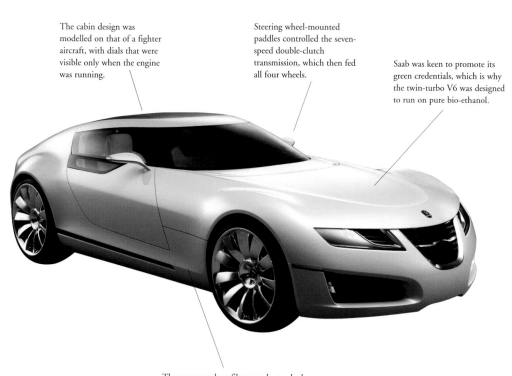

The cabin design was modelled on that of a fighter aircraft, with dials that were visible only when the engine was running.

Steering wheel-mounted paddles controlled the seven-speed double-clutch transmission, which then fed all four wheels.

Saab was keen to promote its green credentials, which is why the twin-turbo V6 was designed to run on pure bio-ethanol.

There were carbon-fibre panels attached to a steel monocoque chassis, for ease of production and strength.

239

SEAT FORMULA

At a time when many manufacturers were embarrassed into being more socially aware, Seat bucked the trend with its Formula concept. It was unveiled as 'bringing the excitement of competition driving to the highway, while not overlooking the comforts needed for more conventional driving'. The reality was that the Formula was just another two-seater roadster – although that didn't make it any less tempting a prospect. Using a 186-kW (250-bhp) 2.0-litre turbocharged petrol engine and six-speed sequential manual gearbox derived from the Cordoba World Rally Car, with the rear wheels doing the driving, the Formula would have been every bit as much fun to drive as the looks promised.

SPECIFICATIONS

ENGINE CAPACITY:	2 litres
CONFIGURATION:	mid-mounted turbo in-line four petrol
POWER:	186 kW (250 bhp)
TOP SPEED:	240 km/h (149 mph)
TRANSMISSION:	six-speed sequential manual, rear-wheel drive
LENGTH:	3943 mm (155.24 in)
WIDTH:	1758 mm (69.21 in)
DEBUT:	Geneva 1999

Following the same back-to-basics theme as the Lotus Elise, Seat's Formula put driving pleasure above absolutely everything else.

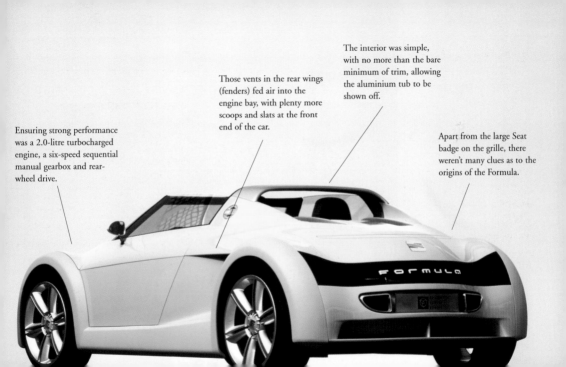

Ensuring strong performance was a 2.0-litre turbocharged engine, a six-speed sequential manual gearbox and rear-wheel drive.

Those vents in the rear wings (fenders) fed air into the engine bay, with plenty more scoops and slats at the front end of the car.

The interior was simple, with no more than the bare minimum of trim, allowing the aluminium tub to be shown off.

Apart from the large Seat badge on the grille, there weren't many clues as to the origins of the Formula.

ᖴᗝᖇᗰᑌᒪᗩ

SIVAX XTILE

Even now you'll struggle to find anybody who has heard of Sivax, yet the Xtile wasn't the first concept to come out of this Japanese company. Two years before this concept was shown, the Kira was unveiled at the 2002 Paris motor show – and the company began working in the automotive sector as long ago as 1964. A compact hatch called the Genos was also displayed at the 1999 Frankfurt motor show, while Sivax has design centres in Europe, China and Japan. Still waiting for the big time, could this be one of the most significant car design companies that nobody has ever heard of?

SPECIFICATIONS

ENGINE CAPACITY:	n/a
CONFIGURATION:	front-mounted petrol
POWER:	n/a
TOP SPEED:	n/a
TRANSMISSION:	n/a
LENGTH:	n/a
WIDTH:	n/a
DEBUT:	Paris 2004

The overall shape of the Xtile worked extremely well, but many of the details were amazingly overcomplicated.

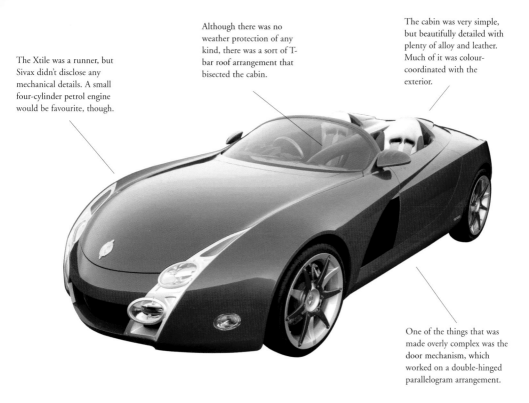

The Xtile was a runner, but Sivax didn't disclose any mechanical details. A small four-cylinder petrol engine would be favourite, though.

Although there was no weather protection of any kind, there was a sort of T-bar roof arrangement that bisected the cabin.

The cabin was very simple, but beautifully detailed with plenty of alloy and leather. Much of it was colour-coordinated with the exterior.

One of the things that was made overly complex was the door mechanism, which worked on a double-hinged parallelogram arrangement.

SUZUKI C2

With its Cappuccino, Suzuki had already proved that it could build a
brilliant small sports car that was fun to drive and cheap to buy.
Despite the success of the car, the C2 never became a production reality –
which was a tragedy because it showed plenty of promise. After the simplicity
of the Cappuccino, Suzuki opted for a more complex car with the C2. With
a 1.6-litre V8 engine, the C2 was unnecessarily complicated under the skin,
yet the interior was simple and the outside was unfussy. Any production car
would have featured a conventional powerplant, but the C2's 186-kW (250-
bhp) 1600-cc V8 offered plenty of low-down torque. Maybe one day …

SPECIFICATIONS

ENGINE CAPACITY:	1600 cc
CONFIGURATION:	front-mounted V8
POWER:	196 kW (250 bhp)
TOP SPEED:	n/a
TRANSMISSION:	six-speed manual, rear-wheel drive
LENGTH:	3650 mm (143.70 in)
WIDTH:	1650 mm (64.96 in)
DEBUT:	Frankfurt 1997

*The C2 was very short and it weighed just 1040 kg
(2293 lb), figures that would have ensured
tremendous agility.*

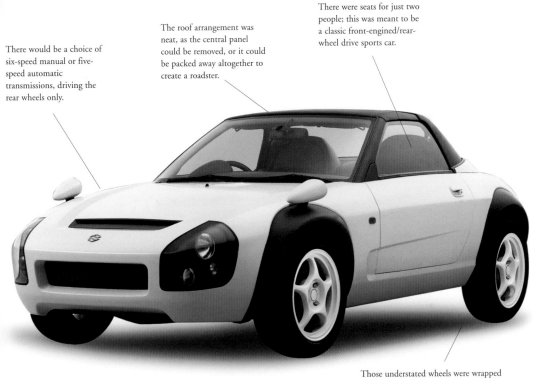

There would be a choice of six-speed manual or five-speed automatic transmissions, driving the rear wheels only.

The roof arrangement was neat, as the central panel could be removed, or it could be packed away altogether to create a roadster.

There were seats for just two people; this was meant to be a classic front-engined/rear-wheel drive sports car.

Those understated wheels were wrapped in 205/50 R16 tyres, while there were disc brakes all round, ventilated at the front.

VOLVO SCC

I f you were asked to name the car maker most likely to build a vehicle
called the Safety Concept Car, the chances are that you'd name Volvo. At
the 2001 Detroit motor show the SCC became a reality, with it making its
debut at a show bristling with new concepts. As the name suggested, the aim
of the SCC was to see how safe it was possible to make a car, without
compromising the ergonomics, aesthetics or dynamics. Indeed, the SCC was
made even safer by making it comfortable as well as making it as good as
possible dynamically – with active safety designed in alongside passive safety.

SPECIFICATIONS

ENGINE CAPACITY:	non-runner
CONFIGURATION:	front-mounted
POWER:	n/a
TOP SPEED:	n/a
TRANSMISSION:	front-wheel drive
LENGTH:	n/a
WIDTH:	n/a
DEBUT:	Detroit 2001
DESIGNER:	Peter Horbury

*The SCC broke away from Volvo's usual boxy
concept styling. Instead there were flowing curves,
with a hint of aggression at the back.*

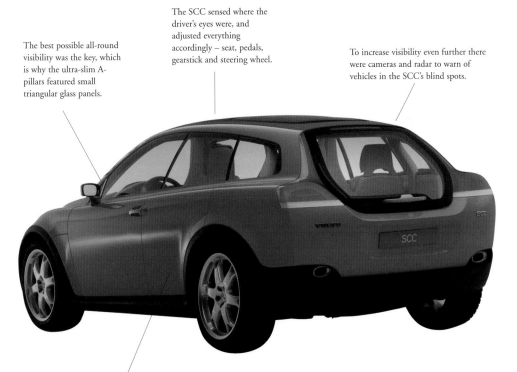

The best possible all-round visibility was the key, which is why the ultra-slim A-pillars featured small triangular glass panels.

The SCC sensed where the driver's eyes were, and adjusted everything accordingly – seat, pedals, gearstick and steering wheel.

To increase visibility even further there were cameras and radar to warn of vehicles in the SCC's blind spots.

The SCC looked as though it was a three-door sporting estate (station wagon), but it was actually equipped with five doors.

EXCESS ALL AREAS

Concept cars should show what's possible when barriers are dropped instead of erected. Only with free thinking can car design truly advance, and these are some of the cars that either move the game on or are just so outrageous that they could never be offered for sale – even if they were to be toned down considerably. All of the cars here pack some of the most advanced technologies imaginable, or simply offer the best of everything – large, powerful engines, lavishly trimmed interiors and plenty of gadgetry. While there will always be a place for ultimate cars, there is room in the marketplace for only so many – and there have generally already been too many from which to choose.

Ever since the first car appeared in the 1880s, designers and engineers have striven to make improvements. There's always room for advancement: more equipment, greater comfort, increases in power or higher levels of safety. These are the cars proving this, but significantly none of them has ever been offered for production. In one or two cases this was considered – but, when you've engineered a car to be built on a money-no-object basis, there will always be very few who can afford it. Still, that should never stop the boundaries from being pushed.

Left: Beautifully impractical, the Pininfarina Rossa was based on the Ferrari 550 Maranello – itself a rare beast.

AUDI AVUS

The Avus brought together Audi's two major selling points: aluminium construction and four-wheel drive. It also launched Audi into a market where it had never been before – that of the mid-engined supercar. However, the Avus was never intended to be a production car – it was created to demonstrate to the world what Audi was capable of. Had the car made its debut a decade later, it may have gone into production – but in 1991 the global economy was in tatters. But it's not all bad news, though. A decade later the Le Mans concept did make its debut – with the news that the car would reach the showrooms.

SPECIFICATIONS

ENGINE CAPACITY:	998 cc
CONFIGURATION:	mid-mounted W12 petrol
POWER:	380 kW (509 bhp)
TOP SPEED:	338 km/h (210 mph)
TRANSMISSION:	six-speed manual, four-wheel drive
LENGTH:	4470 mm (175.98 in)
WIDTH:	2006 mm (78.98 in)
DEBUT:	Tokyo 1991
DESIGNER:	Martin Smith

The interior of the Avus was less flash than the exterior, with a very subtle design but very high quality materials throughout.

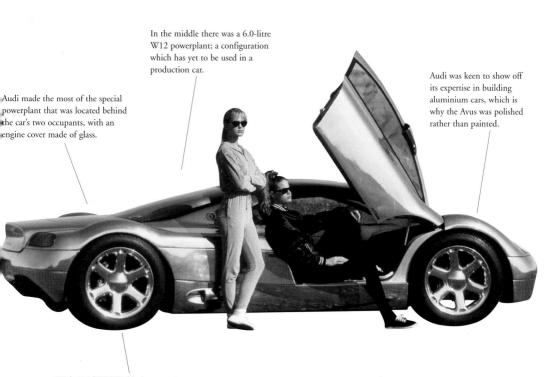

In the middle there was a 6.0-litre W12 powerplant; a configuration which has yet to be used in a production car.

Audi made the most of the special powerplant that was located behind the car's two occupants, with an engine cover made of glass.

Audi was keen to show off its expertise in building aluminium cars, which is why the Avus was polished rather than painted.

With 380 kW (509 bhp) on tap, it was just as well the power went to all four wheels – via Audi's famed quattro system.

BENTLEY HUNAUDIERES

With Lamborghini and Bugatti parts of the Audi stable alongside Bentley, it was no surprise that the Hunaudieres looked like it did; the family resemblance was immediately obvious. This was uncharted territory for Bentley, however, as mid-engined supercars were hardly what it was famed for. Taking its name from the famous Le Mans racing circuit, the Hunaudieres was Audi's way of showing Bentley's independence from Rolls-Royce – something it hadn't enjoyed since 1931 when the two marques merged. That's why it was a technological tour de force, with a massive engine, alloy and carbon-fibre panelling and four-wheel drive. But we got the Continental GT …

SPECIFICATIONS

ENGINE CAPACITY:	8004 cc
CONFIGURATION:	mid-mounted V16
POWER:	465 kW (623 bhp)
TOP SPEED:	320 km/h (200 mph) plus
TRANSMISSION:	five-speed manual, four-wheel drive
LENGTH:	4432 mm (174.49 in)
WIDTH:	1985 mm (78.15 in)
DEBUT:	Geneva 1999

The car had amazing presence, but those tiny projector headlights and large, accentuated grille didn't look right.

Audi was keen for the Hunaudieres to be an ultimate car, which is why it packed a V16 powerplant in the middle.

Helping the 8-litre engine to produce 465 kW (623 bhp) and 761 N m (561 lb ft) of torque were variable valve timing and a quartet of overhead camshafts.

Not only was the mid-engined configuration entirely new for Bentley, but so, too, was the concept of four-wheel drive.

As if the car's lines and proportions weren't dramatic enough, those wheels measured a massive 508 mm (20 in) across.

BUGATTI EB112

There was talk of this car reaching production as long ago as 1994, but, with the demise of Bugatti shortly after, the EB112's fate was sealed. Designed by Giorgetto Giugaro, the EB112 represented Bugatti's attempt at creating the fastest and most luxurious saloon ever made. It was to use a normally aspirated version of the EB110's 3.5-litre twin-turbo V12, enlarged to around six litres. There were five valves per cylinder, while the self-levelling suspension incorporated active ride. Bugatti was too ambitious, however, and, having spent a fortune on a factory that lay idle, the company went bust trying to develop this ultra-exclusive saloon.

SPECIFICATIONS

ENGINE CAPACITY:	5995 cc
CONFIGURATION:	front-mounted V12
POWER:	339 kW (455 bhp)
TOP SPEED:	299 km/h (186 mph)
TRANSMISSION:	six-speed manual, four-wheel drive
LENGTH:	5090 mm (200.39 in)
WIDTH:	1990 mm (78.35 in)
DEBUT:	Geneva 1993

It was easy to see that Giugaro had designed the EB112, with its overtones of the Italdesign Kensington concept.

Although the EB110 featured a twin-turbo V12, the EB112 would have a normally aspirated unit, better suited to a luxury saloon.

From the front the EB112 looked sleek and reasonably stylish; from the back it was bulbous and ungainly.

To keep weight down as much as possible, the bodyshell was made from a combination of carbon fibre and aluminium alloy.

The suspension was cutting edge, with an actively controlled double-wishbone set-up that gave comfort with sharp handling.

255

BUICK Y JOB

This is supposedly the concept that started it all. The reality is that there were plenty of special-bodied cars around before the Y Job was first shown in 1938, but this Buick is generally acknowledged to be the first true concept car. The man responsible was Harley Earl, the first head of design for General Motors. He wanted to push the boundaries of design, to see how far he could go in making GM's cars less like everyone else's, and with the Y Job he achieved exactly that. Based on a stretched Buick Century chassis, the Y Job was much more aerodynamic than contemporaneous production cars.

SPECIFICATIONS

ENGINE CAPACITY:	5245 cc
CONFIGURATION:	front-mounted in-line eight-cylinder petrol
POWER:	105 kW (141 bhp)
TOP SPEED:	n/a
TRANSMISSION:	two-speed auto, rear-wheel drive
LENGTH:	5293 mm (208.39 in)
WIDTH:	1890 mm (74.41 in)
DEBUT:	1938

In 1938, just about every conventional production car was fitted with running boards – but there was none on the Y Job.

There were electrically
operated doors and windows,
which were quite fantastic
for the time.

As with all decent American
cars, there was a 105-kW
(141-bhp) straight-8 engine
under the bonnet (hood), with
a displacement of 5.2 litres.

The door handles and lights
were flush, to make the car
more slippery; there was also
a power-assisted roof.

Even the Dynaflow two-speed automatic
transmission was ahead of its time –
production cars didn't get it until 1948.

CADILLAC CYCLONE

If you lived in America in the 1950s, you were continually surrounded by imagery inspired by the jet age. Nowhere was this more evident than in the world of car design, and especially the concept car. Everywhere you looked there were rocket-shaped over-riders and taillights that looked like the afterburners of a jet engine – and the Cadillac Cyclone typified this approach. With a 6.4-litre V8, the rear wheels were driven via a three-speed automatic gearbox. One of the most amazing touches was the huge glass canopy, which retracted into the boot (trunk) at the touch of a button; it was even coated in vaporized silver to reflect the sun's rays!

SPECIFICATIONS

ENGINE CAPACITY:	6382 cc
CONFIGURATION:	front-mounted V8
POWER:	242 kW (325 bhp)
TOP SPEED:	n/a
TRANSMISSION:	three-speed automatic, rear-wheel drive
LENGTH:	5001 mm (196.89 in)
WIDTH:	n/a
DEBUT:	1959

The Cyclone may have looked as if it should have been propelled by a jet engine, but under the bonnet (hood) was a conventional power unit.

Although the Cyclone now has a conventional windscreen, when unveiled it featured an aeroplane-style canopy.

The running gear was largely conventional, with a three-speed automatic gearbox and a 6.4-litre V8 petrol engine.

Those nose cones weren't just styling affectations; they transmitted radar beams to help avoid crashes in poor visibility.

The doors slid backwards, for entry and exit in confined spaces. Each door had a small panel to pay at toll booths.

259

CADILLAC SIXTEEN

With massively powerful and luxurious concepts being unveiled at every motor show, Cadillac needed to pull out all the stops to produce something that stood out at the 2003 Detroit event. The result was a car that upstaged every other exhibit – and quite rightly so when you consider the car's specification. With a huge V16 engine up front, there were 746 kW (1000 bhp) on tap – although as a token gesture towards the environmentalists there was 'displacement on demand'. This allowed up to 12 of the cylinders to be shut down in a bid to conserve fuel, a feature that's fitted to many of GM's production cars.

SPECIFICATIONS

ENGINE CAPACITY:	13,600 cc
CONFIGURATION:	front-mounted V16 petrol
POWER:	746 kW (1000 bhp)
TOP SPEED:	n/a
TRANSMISSION:	four-speed automatic, rear-wheel drive
LENGTH:	5673 mm (223.25 in)
WIDTH:	2058 mm (81.02 in)
DEBUT:	Detroit 2003
DESIGNER:	Wayne Cherry

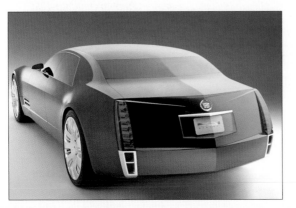

Despite the car having a length of more than 5.5 m (18 ft), the Sixteen's weight was kept down to 2270 kg (5004 lb), thanks to the use of lots of alloy.

There were two V8s stitched together to create a monstrous 13.6-litre V16 unit, which could develop 746 kW (1000 bhp) and 1356 N m (1000 lb ft) of torque.

The interior looked spartan, but was luxuriously equipped with a drinks cabinet, computer terminals and even work tables.

The wheels and tyres were as outrageous as the rest of the car, with 610-mm (24-in) items being fitted at each corner.

Only the rear wheels were driven, while the transmission was a four-speed automatic; Mercedes was building seven-speed units by this time ...

CHRYSLER ATLANTIC

O ne of the most beautiful concept cars ever made, the Chrysler Atlantic was inspired by (and named after) the sublime Bugatti of the same name. Never intended to reach production, this fabulous concept blended classic lines with modern technology. Chrysler, however, cut a few too many corners because, while the Atlantic was fully driveable, so many parts were carried over from the company's regular production cars that piloting it was a hugely disappointing experience. What was much more disappointing, though, was the fact that nothing like this ever made the showrooms at all – which must rate as the biggest waste ever of a design masterpiece.

SPECIFICATIONS

ENGINE CAPACITY:	4.0 litres
CONFIGURATION:	front-mounted straight-eight petrol
POWER:	268 kW (360 bhp)
TOP SPEED:	n/a
TRANSMISSION:	four-speed automatic, rear-wheel drive
LENGTH:	n/a
WIDTH:	n/a
DEBUT:	Detroit 1995
DESIGNER:	Bob Hubbach

The Viper provided a platform on which to base the Atlantic. Sadly, its 8-litre V10 engine wasn't carried over.

Inside was plenty of leather, but no wood. Instead, to bring the car completely up to date, there was lots of carbon-fibre detailing.

As a result of the Atlantic being so poorly developed, its bodyshell would twist every time the throttle was applied.

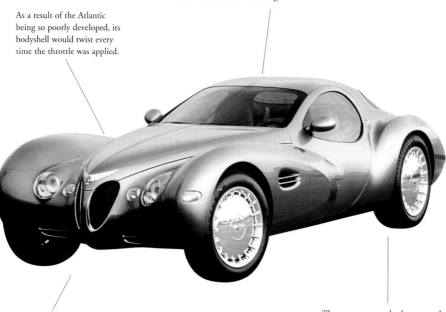

Mimicking the Bugatti Atlantic, there was a straight-eight engine up front, made of two Chrysler Neon units joined together.

Those enormous wheels measured 559 mm (22 in) across, which is why the car was so sluggish; the gearing was too high.

CITROËN ACTIVA 1 & 2

This was the first of two Activa concepts to come from Citroën, with the second one being slightly less radical than the first, both inside and out. While the Activa 2 featured wing (side) mirrors and a fairly conventional interior, the Activa used cameras for rear visibility, while the interior was much more hi-tech. Still, both were true concepts in that they tested designs and technology which Citroën hoped would one day make it into its production cars – and in many cases they already have. With active suspension, safety and comfort gadgetry galore, and radical designs inside and out, Citroën was at last returning its innovative roots.

SPECIFICATIONS

ENGINE CAPACITY:	3 litres
CONFIGURATION:	front-mounted petrol V6
POWER:	164 kW (220 bhp)
TOP SPEED:	n/a
TRANSMISSION:	four-speed auto, four-wheel drive
LENGTH:	4750 mm (187.01 in)
WIDTH:	1900 mm (74.80 in)
DEBUT:	Paris 1988

One of the key technologies the Activa offered was hydropneumatic active suspension, which could be tailored to the driver's requirements.

Four-wheel steering, anti-lock brakes and traction control were all fitted, to keep the driver out of trouble at high speeds.

The rectangular steering wheel never made it onto Citroën's production cars – which is just as well because everybody would have hated it.

A head-up display projected the instrumentation 120 cm (47 in) ahead of the windscreen, so the driver didn't have to take his or her eyes off the road.

By eliminating the B-pillars and adopting rear-hinged back doors, the Activa's cabin could be opened up completely.

FIAT OLTRE

M̲ost of Fiat's concepts over the years have been small cars that are all about clever packaging. Following the then-current fashion for overblown monsters that used as much fuel as possible, however, the Oltre was a bold statement to make in an eco-conscious age. Doing its best to take on the Hummer at its own game, the Oltre was a huge, boxy off-roader that looked as though it had come straight from the heart of a war zone. Based on Iveco's LMV military off-road vehicle, the Oltre could accommodate up to five people – yet weighed an incredible seven tonnes with all its fluids in place!

SPECIFICATIONS

ENGINE CAPACITY:	3000 cc
CONFIGURATION:	front-mounted in-line four-cylinder turbodiesel
POWER:	138 kW (185 bhp)
TOP SPEED:	130 km/h (81 mph)
TRANSMISSION:	six-speed manual, four-wheel drive
LENGTH:	4870 mm (191.73 in)
WIDTH:	2200 mm (86.61 in)

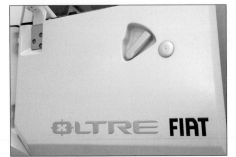

Amusingly, Fiat claimed the Oltre's door handles were flush-fitting so they wouldn't get in the way during off-road manoeuvres.

Although the 3-litre turbodiesel engine wasn't especially powerful, it could develop a very healthy 456 N m (336 lb ft) of torque.

Despite the Oltre's utilitarian nature, it was fitted with high-performance low-profile Pirelli asymmetric 315/40 R26 tyres.

Ground clearance was a generous 50 cm (20 in), which should have enabled just about any terrain to be crossed.

A ford 85 cm (33.5 in) deep could be crossed – or, if extension pipes were added to the intake and exhaust, water up to 1.5 m (five feet) deep could be passed through.

FORD GT90

When Ford came up with New Edge styling, it needed something impressive to show what the theme was all about. It would have been hard to come up with anything more extreme than the GT90, which was a mass of straight edges and sharp lines. It may not have been beautiful, but the GT90 was certainly dramatic – which was in keeping with its claimed top speed of 386 km/h (240 mph). Borrowing many of the mechanical components from the Jaguar XJ220, the GT90 featured a drag coefficient of just 0.32. Still, this figure is pretty much as aerodynamically efficient as it's possible to get with a car of this type.

SPECIFICATIONS

ENGINE CAPACITY: 5927 cc, four turbos
CONFIGURATION: mid-mounted V12 petrol
POWER: 537 kW (720 bhp)
TOP SPEED: 378 km/h (235 mph)
TRANSMISSION: five-speed manual, rear-wheel drive
LENGTH: 4470 mm (175.98 in)
WIDTH: 1963 mm (77.28)
DEBUT: Detroit 1995

The GT90 had an aluminium honeycomb monocoque with carbon-fibre panelling, for the optimum balance between strength and lightness.

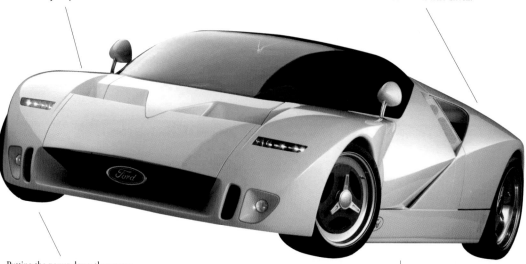

To allow access to the main mechanical components for servicing, the front and rear ends were completely removable.

The five-speed manual gearbox was borrowed from the Jaguar XJ220, while just the rear wheels were driven.

Putting the power down there were 483-mm (19-in) wheels at each corner and rear-wheel drive: four-wheel drive was a possibility.

A 6-litre V12 sat in the middle, complete with four turbochargers – enough to give an astonishing 537 kW (720 bhp).

FORD INDIGO

While concept cars are increasingly sensible with a view to production in some form, the Indigo didn't even try to offer the smallest dose of reality. It looked like a racing car for the road, which is exactly what it was. There was no weather protection and nowhere to stow any luggage, and, with a 6-litre V12 sitting behind the occupants' heads, the purpose of the Indigo was abundantly clear: to go as fast as possible. The Indigo came about thanks to Jacques Villeneuve winning the Indy 500 in a Reynard-Ford; this concept was Ford's way of capitalizing on that success.

SPECIFICATIONS

ENGINE CAPACITY:	5972 cc
CONFIGURATION:	mid-mounted V12 petrol
POWER:	324 kW (435 bhp)
TOP SPEED:	290 km/h (180 mph)
TRANSMISSION:	six-speed sequential manual, rear-wheel drive
LENGTH:	4453 mm (175.31 in)
WIDTH:	2051 mm (80.75 in)
DEBUT:	Detroit 1996
DESIGNER:	Mark Adams/John Hartnell

Attached directly to the back of the Indigo's engine was the transaxle, with the gearchanges activated by buttons on the steering wheel.

The front aerofoil kept the car glued to the Tarmac while also providing somewhere to put the front lights.

An all-aluminium unit with 48 valves and four overhead camshafts, the V12 was capable of producing 324 kW (435 bhp).

Open wheels wouldn't be legal on a road car, so tyre-hugging wheelarches were provided instead, which turned with the wheels.

The V12 engine was based on two V6s stitched together; this unit was later fitted to the Aston Martin DB7 Vantage.

GM FIREBIRDS

All three Firebird concepts were forward-thinking because they each pushed the boundaries of car design. The Firebird I of 1954 was little more than a fighter plane on wheels; it even featured a gas turbine engine and a dorsal fin, along with small wings either side of the fuselage. The plastic bubble canopy was one of the jet-age clichés – one that was repeated on the Firebird II that appeared in 1956. The Firebird II also featured a gas turbine engine and was designed to drive itself. The final car in the series featured twin canopies along with a pair of engines – one was just for the accessories!

SPECIFICATIONS

ENGINE CAPACITY:	n/a
CONFIGURATION:	rear-mounted gas turbine
POWER:	168 kW (225 bhp) (Firebird III)
TOP SPEED:	n/a
TRANSMISSION:	n/a
LENGTH:	n/a
WIDTH:	n/a
DEBUT:	1954, 1956, 1958

All of the Firebirds were fitted with gas turbine engines, which were felt to be the motive power of the future.

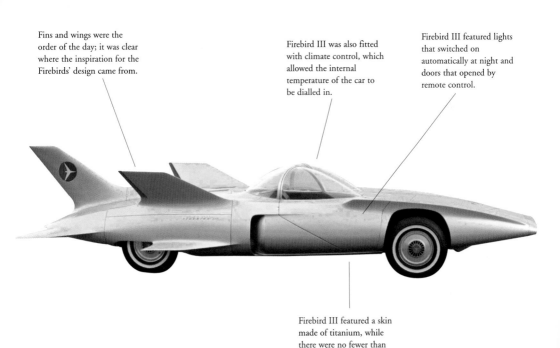

Fins and wings were the order of the day; it was clear where the inspiration for the Firebirds' design came from.

Firebird III was also fitted with climate control, which allowed the internal temperature of the car to be dialled in.

Firebird III featured lights that switched on automatically at night and doors that opened by remote control.

Firebird III featured a skin made of titanium, while there were no fewer than seven fins and wings to maintain high-speed stability.

IAD ALIEN

International Automotive Design was a British design consultancy which decided to make its mark at the 1986 Turin motor show. It would do this by unveiling a non-running concept which would not only be more eye-catching than anything produced by any of the established supercar makers, but would also be more practical and better to drive. The key advance was the way the mechanical components were kept separate from the passenger space, which is why the car had its distinctive tapered body which suddenly widened at the back. The rear-mounted engine was detachable, so that it could be unplugged and replaced with larger or smaller powerplants, depending on the occasion.

SPECIFICATIONS

ENGINE CAPACITY:	non-runner
CONFIGURATION:	mid-mounted
POWER:	n/a
TOP SPEED:	n/a
TRANSMISSION:	n/a
LENGTH:	3696 mm (145.51 in)
WIDTH:	1600 mm (62.99 in)
DEBUT:	Turin 1986
DESIGNER:	Martin Longmore

Although the looks of the Alien were revolutionary, there was much more to the concept than mere aesthetics.

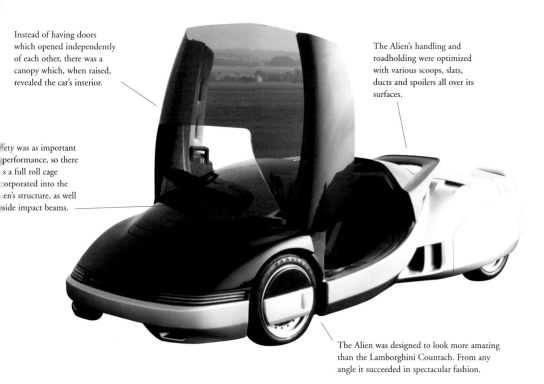

Instead of having doors which opened independently of each other, there was a canopy which, when raised, revealed the car's interior.

The Alien's handling and roadholding were optimized with various scoops, slats, ducts and spoilers all over its surfaces.

fety was as important performance, so there s a full roll cage corporated into the en's structure, as well side impact beams.

The Alien was designed to look more amazing than the Lamborghini Countach. From any angle it succeeded in spectacular fashion.

IDEA ONE

Now there's an inspirational name for a concept – One, or Idea One, as the Italian design house behind it preferred to call it. First shown at the 1999 Geneva motor show, the One was conceived as the ultimate luxury saloon with money being no object. To that end there was a V8 engine in the nose, a lightweight bodyshell for maximum agility and the latest electronics to add comfort and safety into the mix. While the One wasn't intended to go into production, Idea claimed it was fully costed, so that, if somebody wanted to offer it for sale, it would be possible to do so – albeit in very small numbers.

SPECIFICATIONS

ENGINE CAPACITY:	3297 cc
CONFIGURATION:	front-mounted petrol V8
POWER:	265 kW (355 bhp)
TOP SPEED:	249 km/h (155 mph)
TRANSMISSION:	four-speed semiauto, rear-wheel drive
LENGTH:	5162 mm (203.23 in)
WIDTH:	1986 mm (78.19 in)
DEBUT:	Geneva 1999
DESIGNER:	

The car's weight was reduced to a minimum by using an aluminium spaceframe, along with extruded alloy for strengthening.

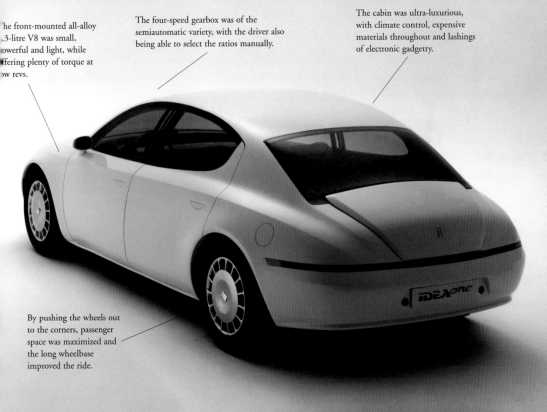

The front-mounted all-alloy 3-litre V8 was small, powerful and light, while offering plenty of torque at low revs.

The four-speed gearbox was of the semiautomatic variety, with the driver also being able to select the ratios manually.

The cabin was ultra-luxurious, with climate control, expensive materials throughout and lashings of electronic gadgetry.

By pushing the wheels out to the corners, passenger space was maximized and the long wheelbase improved the ride.

IDEA one

ITALDESIGN AZTEC

The amount of work that goes into producing a single concept can be astronomical, so it's no surprise that it's rare to see a whole family of concepts unveiled at a motor show. But at the 1988 Turin motor show Italdesign did just that, with a trio of concepts all based on Audi mechanicals. First there was the Asgard, which was a 6 + 2-seater people carrier which put the emphasis on practicality. Then there was the Aspid – a two-seater closed sports car that focused on performance and handling. Effectively it was just a toy, but even more extreme was the open version of the Aspid, called the Aztec.

SPECIFICATIONS

ENGINE CAPACITY:	2226 cc turbocharged
CONFIGURATION:	mid-mounted in-line five-cylinder petrol
POWER:	186 kW (250 bhp)
TOP SPEED:	241 km/h (150 mph)
TRANSMISSION:	five-speed manual, four-wheel drive
LENGTH:	4270 mm (168.11 in)
WIDTH:	1970 mm (77.56 in)
DEBUT:	Turin 1988

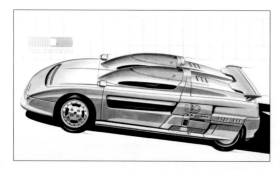

Down each side of the car there was a service centre, which allowed things such as fluid levels to be monitored.

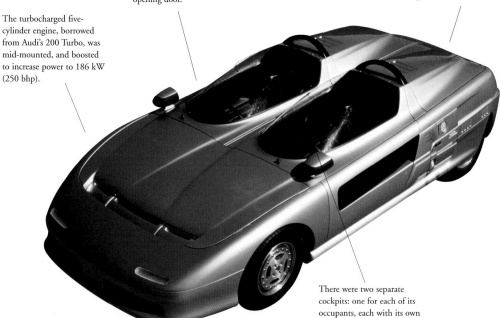

The turbocharged five-cylinder engine, borrowed from Audi's 200 Turbo, was mid-mounted, and boosted to increase power to 186 kW (250 bhp).

The door arrangement was messy, with a separate canopy for each occupant, as well as a conventionally opening door.

Four-wheel drive was becoming fashionable when the Aztec was unveiled. As the car was Audi-based, it was easy to incorporate quattro four-wheel drive.

There were two separate cockpits: one for each of its occupants, each with its own set of instruments.

JEEP HURRICANE

How do you make your concept stand out from the crowd? In the case of the Jeep Hurricane, the answer was to give the car a pair of 5.7-litre V8 engines (one at each end) and wheels that turned in opposite directions to each other so it looked completely mad. Although the Hurricane was meant to be the most powerful and capable Jeep ever, it could also be surprisingly green, thanks to its Multi-Displacement Engine. This could run on 4, 8, 12 or 16 cylinders, depending on power requirements – and the distance of the car from the nearest fuel stop.

SPECIFICATIONS

ENGINE CAPACITY:	5.7 litres x 2
CONFIGURATION:	twin-engined with two V8s
POWER:	500 kW (670 bhp)
TOP SPEED:	n/a
TRANSMISSION:	five-speed auto, four-wheel drive
LENGTH:	3856 mm (151.81 in)
WIDTH:	2033 mm (80.04 in)
DEBUT:	Detroit 2005

The Hurricane was amazingly manoeuvrable thanks to 940-mm (37-in) tyres, 363 mm (14.3 in) of ground clearance and very short overhangs.

As if one 5.7-litre V8 wasn't enough, Jeep put one in the front and another in the back of the Hurricane to give 500 kW (670 bhp).

The Hurricane was instantly recognizable as a Jeep, thanks to classic styling cues such as the seven-bar grille.

Those wheels measured 508 mm (20 in) across and were 254 (10 in) wide; they were wrapped in 305/70 R20 tyres.

To make the Hurricane as manoeuvrable as possible, all four wheels steered so the car could spin on its own axis.

LEXUS 2054

The film *Minority Report* was released in 2002, having been directed by Steven Spielberg and with Harald Belker in charge of vehicle design. To be remotely convincing, the film's creators had to build vehicles that they felt might represent what people would really be driving half a century into the future – the Lexus 2054 concept was the result. This concept was the star of the film, and in some ways this was the very essence of what a concept is all about. It could stretch the boundaries of possibility – and even go beyond. All we have to do now is sit around for a few decades and see how much they got right.

SPECIFICATIONS

ENGINE CAPACITY:	Smart recharging electric engine
CONFIGURATION:	front-mounted
POWER:	500 kW (670 bhp)
TOP SPEED:	n/a
TRANSMISSION:	rear-wheel drive
LENGTH:	3708 mm (145.98 in)
WIDTH:	2083 mm (82.01 in)
DEBUT:	Detroit 2002

There were retractable solar panels that topped up the 2054's batteries and fed the climate control while the car was parked.

The braking system was highly advanced, with ceramic discs at its heart. The system was totally controlled by computer.

The interior was absolutely crammed with gadgetry such as bucket seats that featured automatic heating and cooling.

There weren't any keys to get into the car; instead there was a DNA detection system which also allowed the car to be started.

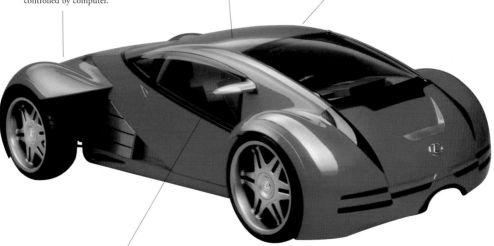

All of the glass incorporated liquid crystal so it could be darkened. Cameras were used instead of mirrors for visibility.

MAYBACH EXELERO

While it looks like a refugee from a Batman film, the Exelero was never designed for a starring role on the silver screen. Instead it was designed as a mobile test bed for high-speed tyres, bankrolled by tyre maker Fulda and based on the platform of the Maybach 57 limousine. This wasn't the first time that Fulda had teamed up with the Maybach marque, nor was it the first time that the tyre maker had built a vehicle specially for the purpose of demonstrating its tyres. Back in 1938, Fulda had paid for a one-off Maybach SW38, to enable high-speed tyre testing on Germany's autobahns.

SPECIFICATIONS

ENGINE CAPACITY:	5908 cc
CONFIGURATION:	front-mounted V12 twin-turbo
POWER:	522 kW (700 bhp)
TOP SPEED:	352 km/h (219 mph)
TRANSMISSION:	five-speed auto, rear-wheel drive
LENGTH:	5890 mm (231.89 in)
WIDTH:	2140 mm (84.25 in)
DEBUT:	Frankfurt 2005

Despite the massive proportions of the Exelero, it was capable of carrying only two people. It was even longer than the Maybach 57.

While the standard Maybach engine isn't exactly lacking, it was reworked to give 522 kW (700 bhp) and 1020 N m (752 lb ft) of torque.

The exhausts exit via the sills, just as they should in any satanic muscle car worth its salt, such as the AC Cobra and Dodge Viper.

The huge grille makes the car look incredibly menacing; it carries strong overtones of Darth Vader's mask, from *Star Wars*.

Those wheels were built specially for the job. Measuring 584 mm (23 in) in diameter, their design is based on that of a turbine.

MERCEDES-BENZ F300 LIFEJET

When Mercedes launched its F300 Life-Jet in 1997, everybody laughed. There was no way anybody would build a car like this; looking like a cross between a motorbike and a car, the three-wheeled contraption featured a narrow body which leaned as the car turned a corner. But in 2003 just such a car did make production – a Dutch vehicle called the Vandenbrink Carver. The F300 was unusually lighthearted for a company as serious as Mercedes – renowned for ideas to make cars safer, more comfortable or more economical. But the F300 wasn't about any of those things – it was unashamedly about putting the fun back into driving.

SPECIFICATIONS

ENGINE CAPACITY: 1598 cc

CONFIGURATION: rear-mounted in-line four-cylinder petrol

POWER: 76 kW (102 bhp)

TOP SPEED: 212 km/h (132 mph)

TRANSMISSION: five-speed sequential manual, rear-wheel drive

LENGTH: 3954 mm (155.67 in)

WIDTH: 1730 mm (68.11 in)

DEBUT: Frankfurt 1997

The F300 was essentially a three-wheeled motorbike, with two seats in tandem. But it drove more like a conventional four-wheeled car.

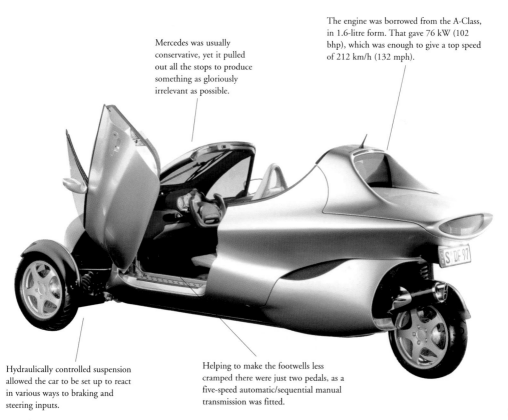

Mercedes was usually conservative, yet it pulled out all the stops to produce something as gloriously irrelevant as possible.

The engine was borrowed from the A-Class, in 1.6-litre form. That gave 76 kW (102 bhp), which was enough to give a top speed of 212 km/h (132 mph).

Hydraulically controlled suspension allowed the car to be set up to react in various ways to braking and steering inputs.

Helping to make the footwells less cramped there were just two pedals, as a five-speed automatic/sequential manual transmission was fitted.

MERCEDES-BENZ C112

During the 1970s Mercedes produced a series of supercar concepts that experimented with different methods of propulsion. They're some of the greatest concepts ever made, as they were true testbeds that covered thousands of miles. Building on the back of this success, Mercedes decided to revive the formula in 1991 with the C112, which was effectively a rolling laboratory. Its purpose was to test new technologies such as traction control, radar distance monitoring, tyre-pressure control and various other active and passive safety systems. While the car itself never went into production, many of the technologies that it was used to develop have since become essential equipment on mainstream cars.

SPECIFICATIONS

ENGINE CAPACITY:	5987 cc
CONFIGURATION:	mid-mounted petrol V12
POWER:	304 kW (408 bhp)
TOP SPEED:	311 km/h (193 mph)
TRANSMISSION:	six-speed manual, rear-wheel drive
LENGTH:	n/a
WIDTH:	n/a
DEBUT:	Frankfurt 1991
DESIGNER:	Bruno Sacco

With a massive 304 kW (408 bhp) on tap, the C112 had an unrestricted top speed of 311 km/h (193 mph). But for political reasons this was capped to 249 km/h (155 mph).

The Active Body Control system featured computer-controlled sensors that adjusted the suspension according to the amount of pitch and roll.

The rear aerofoil was active; it remained static at rest, but could be raised in 0.1 seconds at high speeds, to aid stability.

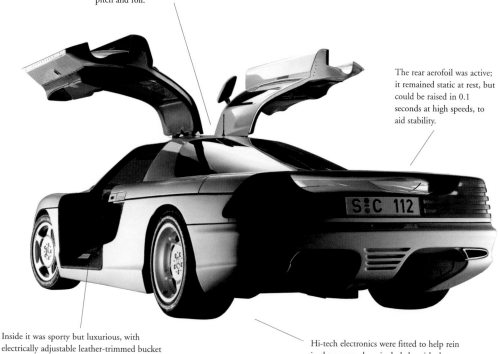

S:C 112

Inside it was sporty but luxurious, with electrically adjustable leather-trimmed bucket seats and a full complement of equipment.

Hi-tech electronics were fitted to help rein in the power; these included anti-lock brakes and anti-skid programmes.

MITSUBISHI ESR

The point of the ESR (Ecological Science Research) was to test the viability of series hybrid personal transport, in which an electric motor and an internal combustion engine worked in harmony to reduce fuel consumption, and hence emissions. To that end, the ESR housed an electric motor at the front, and a turbocharged 1.5-litre petrol engine in the rear. The electric motor would always power the car, but where necessary, the batteries that powered the motor would be charged by the internal combustion engine. In urban environments it ran on battery power alone, but if a boost was needed the petrol engine would cut in to charge up the batteries.

SPECIFICATIONS

ENGINE CAPACITY:	AC induction motor
CONFIGURATION:	front-mounted
POWER:	70 kW (94 bhp)
TOP SPEED:	200 km/h (124 mph)
TRANSMISSION:	three-speed automatic, front-wheel drive
LENGTH:	4535 mm (178.54 in)
WIDTH:	1725 mm (67.91 in)
DEBUT:	Frankfurt 1993

Advances in electric motor technology made the ESR a viable proposition – but at a price that was still too high for production.

The ESR got the best possible efficiency by boosting the engine with a battery-driven powerpack, which was kept charged by the engine.

The petrol engine ran at a constant speed, charging the batteries rather than driving the car. A catalyst kept it clean.

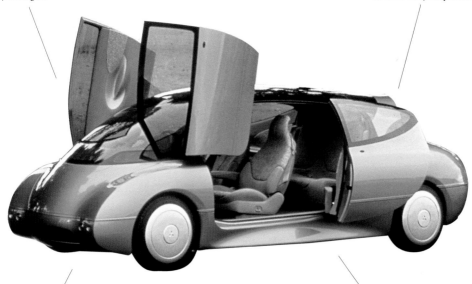

Perhaps one of the ugliest concept cars ever, the ESR looked especially awkward from the rear three-quarters. At least the front was better.

Regenerative braking kept the battery pack topped up. This turned the motor into a generator when engine braking was used.

PEUGEOT QUASAR

Peugeot's designers were clearly smoking illicit substances throughout the 1980s because they came up with the most fantastic trio of concepts. This was the first of the three, with the Proxima and Oxia following later – all as amazing to look at as the Quasar. With large expanses of glass and just two seats, the Quasar had a 447-kW (600-bhp) twin-turbo four-cylinder engine that gave the car the performance to live up to its looks. The cabin was a gadget-lover's dream, with electronic readouts all over the place and a TV screen in front of the driver that displayed warning messages, road maps and even telex messages.

SPECIFICATIONS

ENGINE CAPACITY:	1600 cc twin-turbo
CONFIGURATION:	mid-mounted in-line four-cylinder
POWER:	447 kW (600 bhp)
TOP SPEED:	n/a
TRANSMISSION:	four-wheel drive
LENGTH:	n/a
WIDTH:	n/a
DEBUT:	Paris 1984

It was Clarion that was behind the electronics of the Quasar and its siblings. In 1986 the company showed its own hi-tech concept.

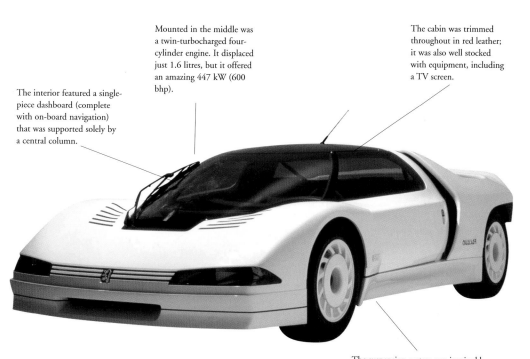

The interior featured a single-piece dashboard (complete with on-board navigation) that was supported solely by a central column.

Mounted in the middle was a twin-turbocharged four-cylinder engine. It displaced just 1.6 litres, but it offered an amazing 447 kW (600 bhp).

The cabin was trimmed throughout in red leather; it was also well stocked with equipment, including a TV screen.

The suspension system was inspired by Formula One engineering, giving the Quasar the handling to go with the looks.

PININFARINA MYTHOS

When you base a concept on a Ferrari Testarossa chassis, there can be only one outcome – a concept supercar which takes the best that the Ferrari had to offer and makes it even better. To that end the 291-kW (390-bhp) 4942-cc flat-12 of the Testarossa was carried over, along with the transmission and suspension, steering and brakes. But whereas the Ferrari wasn't noted for its looks, which were dramatic but not beautiful, the Mythos was certainly a lot more pretty. And while it was claimed that the Mythos would never go into production in any form, certain elements of it would be incorporated into future production Ferraris.

SPECIFICATIONS

ENGINE CAPACITY:	4942 cc
CONFIGURATION:	mid-mounted flat-12 petrol
POWER:	291 kW (390 bhp)
TOP SPEED:	about 257 km/h (160 mph)
TRANSMISSION:	five-speed manual, rear-wheel drive
LENGTH:	4308 mm (169.61 in)
WIDTH:	2108 mm (82.99 in)
DEBUT:	Tokyo 1989
DESIGNER:	Lorenzo Ramaciotti

There wasn't much in the way of exterior decoration, and the inside was much the same, with trim and instrumentation being minimal.

There was 305 mm (12 in) of adjustment available for the rear spoiler; it sat flush at rest, and rose as the car went faster.

The cab-forward stance is most apparent in profile, as is the wedge shape, which has been taken to extremes.

The Testarossa's powerplant was carried over wholesale, with 291 kW (390 bhp). But top speed was just 257 km/h (160 mph) because of the poor aerodynamics.

Those prominent air vents in the rear wings (fenders) provided air for the engine – both to cool it and also to allow it to breathe.

PININFARINA ROSSA

W hile most people would be happy to accept a painting or tankard as a seventieth birthday present, Pininfarina built itself this Ferrari 550 Maranello-based Rossa to commemorate the occasion. With the Rossa wearing prancing-horse badges, its origins were clear – but this car was more minimalist than anything likely to be sold by Ferrari. There was, for example, no weather protection – not even any windscreen wipers. The interior was stripped out, while the two seats were kept apart by a tall central console that stiffened the bodyshell. There were never any plans to produce the Rossa; while it may have been impractical, it would certainly have been fun.

SPECIFICATIONS

ENGINE CAPACITY:	5474 cc
CONFIGURATION:	front-mounted V12
POWER:	362 kW (485 bhp)
TOP SPEED:	299 km/h (186 mph)
TRANSMISSION:	six-speed manual, rear-wheel drive
LENGTH:	4290 mm (168.90 in)
WIDTH:	1940 mm (76.38 in)
DEBUT:	Turin 2000
DESIGNER:	Ken Okuyama

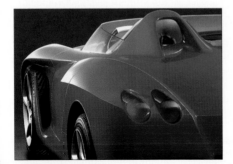

There were no door mirrors. Instead there was a camera that relayed pictures to a dash-mounted screen.

Each occupant got his or her own separate bit of cabin, with a fairing at head height. Access was by electrically operated doors.

The low windscreen meant that, at anything over 64 km/h (40 mph), the car's occupants needed to wear a visor for protection.

Up front there was a 5.5-litre V12, more usually seen in the Ferrari 550 Maranello. That meant there was 362 kW (485 bhp) on tap.

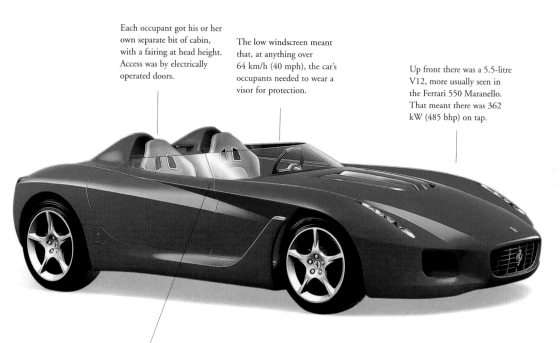

The cabin was simply finished in grey leather, with three hooded gauges finished in anodized alloy facing the driver.

PININFARINA BIRDCAGE

Maserati had a glorious heritage, yet it was always seen as the poor relation to Ferrari. So, to celebrate its seventy-fifth birthday, Pininfarina decided to do an update of a Maserati milestone, creating a Birdcage for the twenty-first century – homage to an icon that was originally born 45 years earlier. The car had to be an ultimate – something that would stop the Geneva motor show when it was unveiled. That meant some pretty radical mechanicals, so what better than those which normally lived under the ultra-exclusive Maserati MC12, itself based on the Ferrari Enzo? Production was never suggested; if it had been, the car would have been guaranteed to sell out.

SPECIFICATIONS

ENGINE CAPACITY:	5998 cc
CONFIGURATION:	mid-mounted V12 petrol
POWER:	522 kW (700 bhp)
TOP SPEED:	322 km/h (200 mph) plus
TRANSMISSION:	six-speed semiauto, rear-wheel drive
LENGTH:	4656 mm (183.31 in)
WIDTH:	2020 mm (79.53 in)
DEBUT:	Geneva 2005

The Birdcage's low height is accentuated by the massive wheels which measure 508 mm (20 in) across at the front and 559 mm (22 in) at the back.

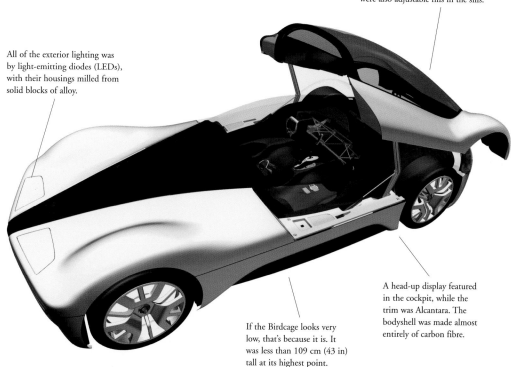

The whole of the back of the car was dominated by a massive diffuser, while there were also adjustable fins in the sills.

All of the exterior lighting was by light-emitting diodes (LEDs), with their housings milled from solid blocks of alloy.

If the Birdcage looks very low, that's because it is. It was less than 109 cm (43 in) tall at its highest point.

A head-up display featured in the cockpit, while the trim was Alcantara. The bodyshell was made almost entirely of carbon fibre.

PININFARINA CHRONOS

Although the Chronos wasn't a runner when it was first shown at the 1991 Geneva motor show, it didn't take long to develop the car into more than a mere static exhibit. With its 281-kW (377-bhp) twin-turbo Lotus Carlton powerplant, complete with a six-speed manual gearbox, the Chronos promised massive performance, as it weighed a whopping 200 kg (440 lb) less than the car it was based upon – and that could do 285 km/h (177 mph). Although Pininfarina was keen to get GM to put the car into production (it even had the factory capacity to do so), the US corporation probably felt it was too close to its own Corvette for comfort.

SPECIFICATIONS

ENGINE CAPACITY:	3615 cc twin-turbo
CONFIGURATION:	front-mounted in-line six-cylinder petrol
POWER:	281 kW (377 bhp)
TOP SPEED:	306 km/h (190 mph)
TRANSMISSION:	six-speed manual, rear-wheel drive
LENGTH:	4320 mm (170.08 in)
WIDTH:	1880 mm (74.02 in)
DEBUT:	Geneva 1991

The whole of the top half of the Chronos was made of glass; this would have used liquid crystal to control cabin temperatures.

It looked as though the engine should have been in the middle, but it was actually located in the nose, just like in the donor car.

The lightweight roof was held in place by four clips. Once removed, it could be stored in the rear of the body tub.

The interior was largely non-functioning. What was there was minimal, with the bucket seats tailored in tan leather trim.

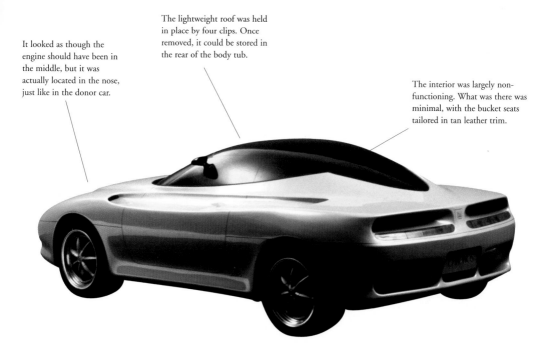

RINSPEED EGO ROCKET

Y̲ou can always rely on Rinspeed to come up with something completely
irrelevant at each year's Geneva motor show. The company has a long-
standing tradition of coming up with the most outrageous concepts, none of
which ever has any chance of production. In a way, this is what concepts
should be about, as Rinspeed's efforts really push the boundaries. Looking
like a pre-war Mercedes or Auto Union racer, the Ego Rocket was actually
inspired by the Bonneville salt flats speed-record cars of the 1940s. A
development of the previous year's Mono Ego, this concept was initially
offered for production, though no further copies were made.

SPECIFICATIONS

ENGINE CAPACITY:	4601 cc supercharged
CONFIGURATION:	mid-mounted petrol V8
POWER:	306 kW (410 bhp)
TOP SPEED:	261 km/h (162 mph)
TRANSMISSION:	five-speed manual
LENGTH:	4267 mm (167.99 in)
WIDTH:	1803 mm (70.98 in)
DEBUT:	Geneva 1998

*As with all Rinspeed concepts, the Ego
Rocket was built as a collaboration.
Continental produced the tyres, with
wheels by Antera.*

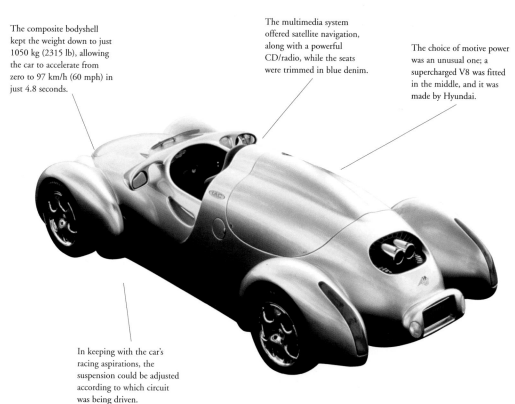

The composite bodyshell kept the weight down to just 1050 kg (2315 lb), allowing the car to accelerate from zero to 97 km/h (60 mph) in just 4.8 seconds.

The multimedia system offered satellite navigation, along with a powerful CD/radio, while the seats were trimmed in blue denim.

The choice of motive power was an unusual one; a supercharged V8 was fitted in the middle, and it was made by Hyundai.

In keeping with the car's racing aspirations, the suspension could be adjusted according to which circuit was being driven.

RINSPEED ADVANTIGE R1

Although it was clearly inspired by racing car design, the Advantige R1 was intended to be an environmentally friendly sports car, thanks to its motive power being supplied by an engine that burned compressed natural gas. Although conventional petrol could also be used, the attraction of the Advantige R1 was that it could be fuelled by garden or kitchen waste. That allowed the car to produce up to 95 per cent fewer exhaust emissions, while it was also claimed that it was carbon neutral. Most importantly for Rinspeed, though, this was the company's way of introducing its new Advantige tuning brand for Audi products.

SPECIFICATIONS

ENGINE CAPACITY:	1795 cc
CONFIGURATION:	rear-mounted in-line four-cylinder biofuel
POWER:	89 kW (120 bhp)
TOP SPEED:	204 km/h (127 mph)
TRANSMISSION:	five-speed manual, rear-wheel drive
LENGTH:	3912 mm (154.02 in)
WIDTH:	1828 mm (71.97 in)
DEBUT:	Geneva 2001

As with all true racing cars, the driver sat in the middle, as the Advantige R1 was strictly a single-seater only.

It's no wonder the car looks low; at just 97 cm (38 in) tall, this was the world's lowest car according to Rinspeed.

The cabin could be moved relative to the rest of the car, by a series of electric motors, for better visibility in urban driving.

A head-up display meant the driver didn't have to take his or her eyes off the road to check the instrumentation.

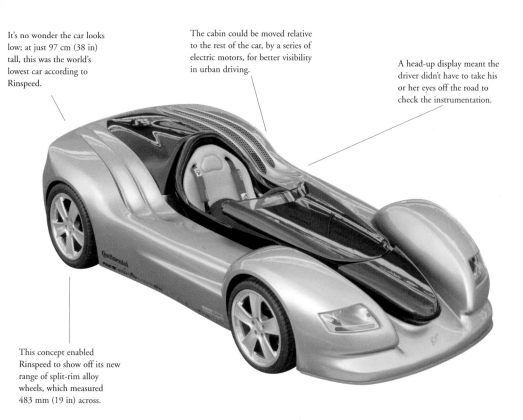

This concept enabled Rinspeed to show off its new range of split-rim alloy wheels, which measured 483 mm (19 in) across.

SHELBY GR-1

With plenty of red ink on the balance sheet and little sign of improvement, Ford needed to come up with an image boost – and fast. So in 2005 it unveiled an alloy-bodied supercar in the vein of the brutal AC Cobra – something that could take on the Dodge Viper and beat it at its own game. Packing a 415-kW (605-bhp) V10 engine in its nose, the Shelby GR-1 was a fully engineered working prototype that Ford reckoned may well have seen production. It was obvious, however, that such a vehicle would only ever sit on the sidelines while more important models made Ford its money – so the project bit the dust.

SPECIFICATIONS

ENGINE CAPACITY:	6392 cc
CONFIGURATION:	front-mounted V10 petrol
POWER:	415 kW (605 bhp)
TOP SPEED:	322 km/h (200 mph)
TRANSMISSION:	six-speed manual, rear-wheel drive
LENGTH:	4412 mm (173.70 in)
WIDTH:	1895 mm (74.61 in)
DEBUT:	Detroit 2005

The body panels were all made of aluminium, which is why Ford took the opportunity to show the car in its naked, polished state.

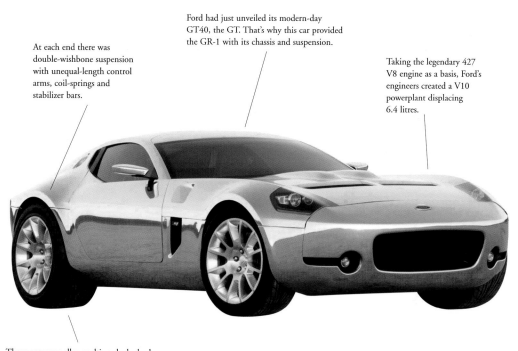

Ford had just unveiled its modern-day GT40, the GT. That's why this car provided the GR-1 with its chassis and suspension.

At each end there was double-wishbone suspension with unequal-length control arms, coil-springs and stabilizer bars.

Taking the legendary 427 V8 engine as a basis, Ford's engineers created a V10 powerplant displacing 6.4 litres.

Those gorgeous alloy multi-spoked wheels measured 483 mm (19 in) in diameter; behind were 356-mm (14-in) brake discs at the front.

TOYOTA FXS

Proving that you *can* have too much of a good thing, the FXS was one of 17 Toyota concepts unveiled at the 2001 Tokyo motor show. Despite its 4.3-litre V8 and impractical two-seater roadster configuration, the FXS was actually quite a sensible car, even if it did appear to be pretty way out. In keeping with the practice of giving its concepts a design theme, Toyota reckoned the FXS featured a 'simple and sexy form with a sense of presence'. That was a vaguely understandable brief – but from the front the FXS bore a close resemblance to the Batmobile from the film *Batman Forever*.

SPECIFICATIONS

ENGINE CAPACITY:	4293 cc
CONFIGURATION:	front-mounted V8 petrol
POWER:	210 kW (282 bhp)
TOP SPEED:	n/a
TRANSMISSION:	six-speed sequential manual, rear-wheel drive
LENGTH:	4150 mm (163.39 in)
WIDTH:	1870 mm (73.62 in)
DEBUT:	Tokyo 2001

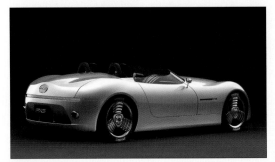

Looking like no Toyota you've seen before, the FXS was a runner so it could enter production in one form or another.

Strong performance was guaranteed, with a 4.3-litre V8. That gave zero to 100 km/h (62 mph) in little more than six seconds and a top speed of up to 249 km/h (155 mph).

Practicality wasn't high on the list of priorities for the FXS – there was no weather protection and there was seating for just two people.

There were plenty of flashes of brilliance, such as the strip headlights, gaping front grilles and the curved aeroscreen.

The interior was radical, with blue-backlit instruments and what appeared to be a small post-war jukebox on the fascia.

VOLKSWAGEN W12

When the W12 made its debut, Volkswagen claimed it was a one-off, but the car could be made available in limited numbers. Most commentators thought the car was fantastic – but the Volkswagen badges didn't help. Perhaps that was enough to scupper the project, but it didn't die very quickly because at the 1998 Geneva motor show a roadster version was unveiled and at the 2002 Geneva motor show both Italdesign and Volkswagen had a W12 coupé on their stands. But soon after it was revealed the project was dead – VW/Audi had enough supercars with the Bugatti Veyron as well as two new Lamborghinis (the Murciélago and Gallardo).

SPECIFICATIONS

ENGINE CAPACITY:	5584 cc
CONFIGURATION:	mid-mounted W12, petrol
POWER:	313 kW (420 bhp)
TOP SPEED:	257 km/h (160 mph)
TRANSMISSION:	six-speed manual, four-wheel drive
LENGTH:	4400 mm (173.23 in)
WIDTH:	1920 mm (75.59 in)
DEBUT:	Tokyo 1997

With its mid-mounted W12 engine, this Volkswagen would have been one of the fastest ever supercars if it had entered production.

The domed roof followed the VW corporate look seen on the Beetle and Passat. But they didn't have the W12's beetle-wing doors!

Helping to keep the weight down, the bodyshell was made of Kevlar. That made it expensive, but incredibly strong and light.

Those 483-mm (19-in) alloy wheels made the car look sleek, fast and expensive – especially when wrapped in ultra-low profile rubber.

Power went to all four wheels. With 313 kW (420 bhp), the W12 needed to be as usable as possible, even in the wet.

311

VOLKSWAGEN GX3

It may have looked pretty mad to have come from a company as conservative as Volkswagen, but the GX3 was briefly considered for production. Built as a fully engineered working prototype, the GX3 would inject some excitement into the VW brand – but the thinking was that it might have injected just a bit too much excitement. According to VW, with just three wheels and the bare minimum of crash or weather protection, the car would take too much engineering to make it safe for lawsuit-happy Americans who would probably end up bankrupting the company when they rolled the car, then sued for damages.

SPECIFICATIONS

ENGINE CAPACITY:	1.6 litres
CONFIGURATION:	rear-mounted in-line four-cylinder petrol
POWER:	93 kW (125 bhp)
TOP SPEED:	201 km/h (125 mph)
TRANSMISSION:	six-speed manual, rear-wheel drive
LENGTH:	3753 mm (147.76 in)
WIDTH:	1850 mm (72.83 in)
DEBUT:	Los Angeles 2006

The GX3 was short for g-forces crossover three-wheeler. Perhaps a GX4 may have been more suitable for production.

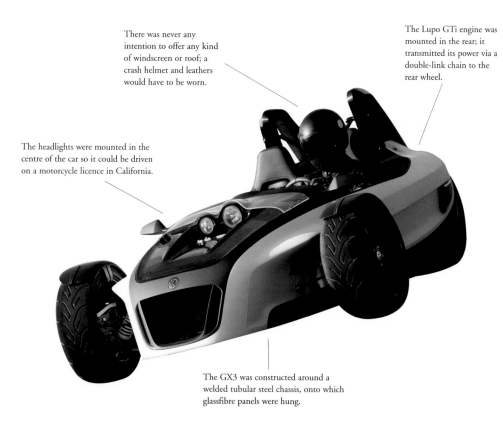

There was never any intention to offer any kind of windscreen or roof; a crash helmet and leathers would have to be worn.

The Lupo GTi engine was mounted in the rear; it transmitted its power via a double-link chain to the rear wheel.

The headlights were mounted in the centre of the car so it could be driven on a motorcycle licence in California.

The GX3 was constructed around a welded tubular steel chassis, onto which glassfibre panels were hung.

ZAGATO RAPTOR

B obsleigh champion Alain Wicki approached Italian design house Zagato to produce a dramatic supercar based on the Lamborghini Diablo VT, with a view to putting the car into limited production if the demand was there. When the car made its debut at the 1996 Geneva motor show it was greeted enthusiastically by the press and public alike, and by the time the show closed there were 550 people who had expressed an interest in buying one. The problem was that Lamborghini was going through major changes at the time, and as a result the project faltered. In the end there was just the one prototype built.

SPECIFICATIONS

ENGINE CAPACITY:	5707 cc
CONFIGURATION:	mid-mounted V12 petrol
POWER:	367 kW (492 bhp)
TOP SPEED:	322 km/h (200 mph)
TRANSMISSION:	five-speed manual, four-wheel drive
LENGTH:	4380 mm (172.44 in)
WIDTH:	2020 mm (79.53 in)
DEBUT:	Geneva 1996
DESIGNER:	Norihiko Harada

Base a concept on the Lamborghini Diablo and you can't fail to produce something that looks like a million dollars.

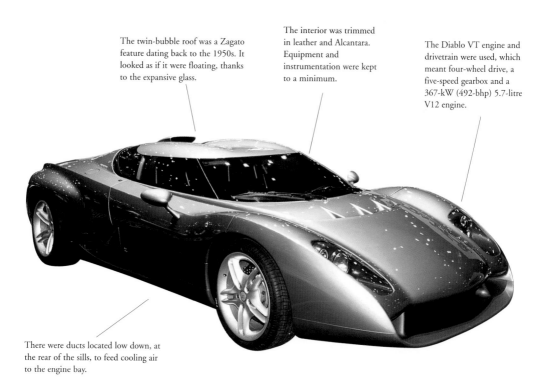

The twin-bubble roof was a Zagato feature dating back to the 1950s. It looked as if it were floating, thanks to the expansive glass.

The interior was trimmed in leather and Alcantara. Equipment and instrumentation were kept to a minimum.

The Diablo VT engine and drivetrain were used, which meant four-wheel drive, a five-speed gearbox and a 367-kW (492-bhp) 5.7-litre V12 engine.

There were ducts located low down, at the rear of the sills, to feed cooling air to the engine bay.

ZENDER FACT 4

Better known for its car styling kits, German tuning company Zender also produced a series of concept cars during the 1980s and 1990s aimed at promoting the company's wares. Following on from where the Vision 3 left off, the Fact 4 offered much the same as the other cars in the series: a huge engine in an aggressively styled lightweight bodyshell. Using an Audi V8 engine with a pair of turbochargers strapped on, the Fact 4 was intended to be a supercar of the highest order; with a top speed of somewhere around 300 km/h (187 mph), it certainly had the performance – as well as the looks.

SPECIFICATIONS

ENGINE CAPACITY:	3562 cc twin-turbo
CONFIGURATION:	mid-mounted petrol V8
POWER:	334 kW (448 bhp)
TOP SPEED:	301 km/h (187 mph)
TRANSMISSION:	five-speed manual, rear-wheel drive
LENGTH:	4080 mm (160.63 in)
WIDTH:	2000 mm (78.74 in)
DEBUT:	Frankfurt 1989

The key to the Fact 4's strength and light weight was a carbon-fibre monocoque. Consequently the car weighed just 1110 kg (2447 lb).

The interior was much like that of a race car's, with carbon-fibre bucket seats and the bare minimum of gadgetry.

ounted in the
ddle was an
di V8, with a
r of KKK
bochargers and
ercoolers to give
4 kW (448 bhp).

Only the rear wheels were driven, with a five-speed gearbox transmitting the huge 529 N m (390 lb ft) of torque from the V8.

The wheels measured 432 mm (17 in) across; they were 254 mm (10 in) wide at the front and 305 mm (12 in) wide at the rear.

Index